D1146758

Authority in Heaven; Authority on Earth

*Principalities and Powers, Binding and Loosing,
Defensive Spiritual Warfare*

Tom Marshall

Sovereign World

Sovereign World Ltd
PO Box 777
Tonbridge
Kent TN11 0ZS
England

Copyright © 2005 Tom Marshall

All rights reserved. No part of this publication may be reproduced, stored
in a retrieval system, or transmitted in any form or by any means, electronic,
mechanical, photocopying, recording or otherwise, without the prior written
consent of the publisher.

Short extracts may be quoted for review purposes.

Scripture quotations, unless otherwise indicated, are taken from
The HOLY BIBLE, NEW INTERNATIONAL VERSION.
Copyright © 1973, 1978, 1984 by International Bible Society.
Used by permission of Hodder and Stoughton Limited.

Other versions used are:

NKJV – New King James Version. Copyright © 1982 by Thomas Nelson, Inc.
Used by permission. All rights reserved.

RSV – Revised Standard Version. Copyright © 1946, 1952 by the Division of
Christian Education of the National Council of the Churches of Christ in the
United States of America.

AV – Authorised (King James) Version. Crown Copyright.

ASB – American Standard Version of the Bible. Copyright © 1960, 1962,
1963, 1968, 1975, 1977, The Lockman Foundation, La Habra, California.

NASB – Copyright © 1960, 1962, 1963, 1968, 1971, 1972, 1973, 1975, 1977,
1995, The Lockman Foundation, La Habra, California.

ISBN: 1 85240 439 6

The publishers aim to produce books which will help to extend and build up
the Kingdom of God. We do not necessarily agree with every view expressed
by the author, or with every interpretation of Scripture expressed. We expect
each reader to make his/her judgment in the light of their own understanding
of God's Word and in an attitude of Christian love and fellowship.

Cover design by CCD, www.ccdgroup.co.uk
Typeset by CRB Associates, Reepham Norfolk
Printed in the United States of America

Publisher's Note

The contents of this book were originally produced as three separate booklets as part of the **Explaining Series** produced by Sovereign World Ltd.

Tom Marshall was a well respected and gifted teacher and by combining these teachings on related subjects it is hoped that they will be helpful to a wider audience in a consolidated form.

The original books have been kept separate but follow on from each other, although there is inevitably some overlap in content.

Contents

SECTION 1

Principalities and Powers

Introduction

As Christians we are continually aware that we live in a fallen world that is unfavorable to the Gospel and often actively antagonistic to it.

In the secular spheres of society, in the realms of business, commerce, politics and entertainment, we are conscious of a self-confident ruthlessness and a hedonistic godlessness that often intimidate us. On Sunday in church we may sing the victorious hymns of Zion and militant songs about "taking the land", but if we are honest we will admit that in the workplace on Monday morning most of us feel almost totally helpless.

In Ephesians 6:12 Paul identifies the locus of the conflict as follows:

> *"For our struggle is not against flesh and blood, but against the rulers, against the authorities, against the powers of this dark world and against the spiritual forces of evil in the heavenly realms."*

If we are to be the overcomers we are meant to be, we need to know:

☐ the true characteristics of the conflict we face,

☐ the nature of the "land" we are meant to take, and

☐ the real identity of the enemies that oppose us.

More importantly, we must understand that **the source of our victory is the death of Jesus Christ on the Cross and His resurrection from the dead**, or what the Bible calls the *"blood of the Lamb"* (Revelation 12:11). But to face the powers with confidence we must really know how and why the Cross has such awesome power. These are the topics that we will address in the pages that follow.

An Overview
of the Battlefield

We have, as it were, arrived on this earthly scene to find ourselves in the middle of a spiritual battle, one moreover in which there are no exempt civilians and no neutral territories. Therefore we need to be clear first of all as to what is going on and why, and second, what our place is in the conflict.

The Bible reveals the existence of a cosmic conflict between God and Satan in which the battlefield is this earth and the human race. **At issue is Satan's attempt to separate God from His creation word**, that is, God's declared intent and purpose to have:

■ Man in His image, after His likeness and having dominion (Genesis 1:27–28);

■ The whole earth filled with His glory (Numbers 14:21; Habakkuk 2:14);

■ All things in heaven and on earth together under the headship of Christ (Ephesians 1:10).

To get the right perspective on the form that this struggle has taken we need to go back to the beginnings, that is to creation and the Fall.

Creation

All creation, Paul tells us, is Christ centered, He is its source, its architect and its end.

> *"For by Him all things were created, both in the heavens and on earth, visible and invisible, whether thrones or dominions or rulers or authorities – all things have been created through Him and for Him. He is before all things, and in Him all things hold together."* (Colossians 1:16–17, NASB)

> *"For from him and through him and to him are all things."* (Romans 11:36)

When we ask, "What is outside the 'all things' of creation?", the answer is, "nothing". When we ask "What is included in the 'all things' of creation?", we can distinguish the following three important categories:

1. *Reality structured in two dimensions or realms.*

    (a) The spiritual realm and within it the angelic/demonic orders.

    (b) The material realm and within it the orders of nature.

2. *Mankind inhabiting both the material and the spiritual realm.*

3. *The things that mankind has created*; that is, cultures, societies, organizations, institutions, constructions, technologies, sciences, art etc.

The creation mandate
The biblical destiny of mankind is set out in what is called the creation mandate, sometimes the dominion mandate or

the cultural mandate. It is the charge God gave to mankind to steward the created earth and unfold its meaning.

> *"God blessed them and said to them, 'Be fruitful and increase in number; fill the earth and subdue it. Rule over the fish of the sea and the birds of the air and over every living creature that moves on the ground.'"* (Genesis 1:28)

The creation mandate had two enabling commands:

1. *Be fruitful and increase*, and

2. *Rule over the earth.*

The family

The first of these commands began to be fulfilled with the beginning of the human family (Genesis 4:1). The importance of the family and the reason for the constant satanic pressure and attack on the family lies in the fact that it is a divinely ordained institution that has to do with man's destiny in relation to the earth.

The city

The second enabling command began to be fulfilled in the building of the first city.

> *"Cain lay with his wife, and she became pregnant and gave birth to Enoch. Cain was then building a city, and he named it after his son Enoch."* (Genesis 4:17)

Henceforth all Bible history centers on cities. The names of some are household words when we think of biblical topics – Babylon and Nineveh, Tyre and Sidon, Sodom and Gomorrah, Rome and Jerusalem, Damascus, Samaria, Jericho, Antioch, Athens and Caesarea Philippi. There are also dozens of others whose names are unfamiliar and strange and whose significance we no longer understand.

It is to the **inner history of the city** that we have to turn in the next chapter but we need to understand its importance to the whole of our present study. Note the following points to which we will return in more detail later.

■ The city is the enduring symbol throughout Scripture for what man corporately creates. Thus:

☐ *At the macro level* it stands in political terms for the state or the nation, and in sociological terms for the entire culture of a nation or people. The first states were city states and the major empires of antiquity. For example the Babylonian, Assyrian and Roman empires were founded on cities; when the city fell, the empire fell.

☐ *At the micro level* the city also stands as a symbol for all the individual structures within a state or society. For example, a business corporation, a school, a town council, a club, or even a local church, are in every sense of the word, little "cities".

■ The symbol of the city in the Old Testament stands for the same realities that are termed in the New Testament the *principalities and powers*, in all their various manifestations – thrones, dominions, rulers and authorities. These all recognizable in our modern society in exactly the same operations.

☐ *Thrones* are the symbolic ways of expressing the authority invested in an office that is continuous over time regardless of its current occupant. We speak of the "bench", for the authority of the law court judges, the "chair" for the one presiding at a meeting, the "oval office" for the presidency of the United States or "No. 10 Downing Street" for the office of Prime Minister in Britain. They are all thrones.

☐ *Dominions* are the spheres of influence over which thrones preside or hold sway. It may be visible – the territory of a State government, or the city limits for example; or invisible – as when we speak of "the power of the press".

☐ *Rulers* are the incumbents holding the office, that is, the investiture of power in a person. It is therefore not the person as such, but the person-in-office; for example, not just John Brown but Mayor John Brown is a ruler.

☐ *Authorities* are the legitimations and sanctions by which authority is maintained, such as laws, regulations, rules, codes and constitutions, both written and customary.

The Fall

In the Fall, not only does mankind sin, but the dominion mandate turns against God.

■ ***Man builds his cities as the expression of his destiny to rule, but he does it in rebellion***. Thus the city Babel becomes the expression of man's corporate rebellion against God, a rebellion so ominous that it brought divine intervention (Genesis 11:1–9).

■ ***Man loses his spiritual authority over creation***. Into the power vacuum thus created Satan comes and establishes his demonic principalities and powers in the heavenly realm. These powers likewise appear in association with the city in the Old Testament. The Hebrew word for "city" also means "the watching angel", thus behind the structural power of the city we find the watching angel, the demon god of the city. The Bible names many of them – Baal, Dagon, Timmutz, Moloch,

Ashtoreth, Chemosh, Adrammalech, Diana, Rimmon, Nergal and others.

Rebellion

In the Fall, God therefore faces rebellion against His will at three levels:

☐ *Level 1*: The individual rebellion of fallen men and women.

☐ *Level 2*: The corporate rebellion of the city, the fallen structures.

☐ *Level 3*: The satanic rebellion of the demonic powers.

Level 1 is the **realm of flesh and blood**. Levels 2 and 3 are the **realm of spirit**, and it is essential we distinguish them, both from Level 1 and from each other.

Turn again to Ephesians 6:12 where it is clearly expressed:

☐ *Level 1*: *"For our struggle is not against flesh and blood..."*

☐ *Level 2*: *"but against the rulers, against the authorities, against the powers of this dark world..."*

☐ *Level 3*: *"and against the spiritual forces of evil in the heavenly realms."*

The importance of this understanding will emerge as we go on.

The City and the Structural Powers

In the Old Testament, almost as soon as the city appears it becomes a major factor in human history. Civilization, culture, learning, and technology flourish in the city. It becomes the magnet for wealth, economic power, political influence and colonization, but it also becomes the focus of military power, conquest, slavery and oppression and the center of idolatry and the occult. It is important to see why and how this is so because we now live in the age of the mega city and the super power. The city has grown to gigantic stature.

The city is named

From its beginning with Cain the city is always named. In the Bible, names always express character or identity, therefore the city once named also acquires a distinctive character. Thus Nineveh is *"the mistress of sorceries"* (Nahum 3:4), Tyre is *"the city of revelry"* (Isaiah 23:7), Babylon *"the mother of prostitutes"* (Revelation 17:5), and Damascus *"the city of renown"* (Jeremiah 49:25).

It is the same today. London has a character that distinguishes it from Paris or Sydney, Berne is different from Seoul, New York is unlike Chicago and so on. Even a corporation or a church has its own individual culture or character that is immediately noticed by newcomers.

The city becomes a power

This is a very important concept to grasp. A city (or a company or an institution), is created by, and lives through the corporate decisions of men and women, each of whom has a human spirit. When this corporate entity begins to function as such, there eventually comes into being a corporate spirit that embodies the character or personality of the organization and gives it its individuality and distinctiveness. This corporate spirit or persona becomes a created reality in its own right. It is distinct from the people who at any time make up the inhabitants or members of the city. For example, what is London? It is not the people who now live in London, because 100 years ago none of them were born but London was there. In 100 years time none of the present inhabitants of London will be alive, but London will be alive and well.

Although it calls it "a legal fiction" the legal system recognizes something like this when it treats a registered company as a separate entity from the shareholders who own it. The company can sue its own shareholders and in turn be sued by them, and even if all the shareholders die the company remains in existence.

Here are some of the features of this corporate spirit or personality of the city:

■ *Although it is created by its founders, the city becomes increasingly independent of them*. Instead of being shaped by people, it shapes them; it develops its own inner culture and ways of functioning to which people have to conform. This is true of a business corporation, a college, a government department, a football club, or a church. In the case of a church it is this corporate spirit or personality that in the letters to the seven churches in the book of Revelation is called the "angel" of the church (Revelation 1:20; 2:1, 8, 12, 18; 3:1, 7, 14).

■ *Although its character is originally malleable and able to be shaped, the corporate spirit of the city becomes increasingly set in its ways and resistant to change.* Thus characteristically an established church always resists renewal, and a culture never changes without upheaval and trauma.

■ *Originally created to serve the people, the city ends up using the people to serve its own ends.* Whether in the form of a corporation or a service club or a church, the "it" demands loyalty, commitment and obedience, and rewards those who serve it well.

■ *Its predominant instinct is for survival.* Babylon, the city says to itself, *"I will continue for ever – the eternal queen! . . . I will never be a widow or suffer the loss of children"* (Isaiah 47:7, 8). People live and die, the city endures, staff come and go, the corporation goes on in perpetuity. Under threat it will use any means to survive and pay any price to maintain itself in existence.

The city is fallen

Because the "it" is created by fallen men, the city is also fallen, and, with Babel, becomes the expression of man's corporate rebellion against God (Genesis 11:1–9). But note the following important points:

■ *The city in itself is not demonic, but it is fallen*, that is to say it does some good things but also some evil things, it has legitimate ends but also strives for sinful and illegitimate ends.

■ *One mark of the city's fallenness is its drive to become idolatrous*, in other words it strives to be the ultimate value in people's lives and claims ultimate authority over them. It wants its interests to come before family, before personal interests, before health, before God.

God says,

> *"I am God, and there is no other;*
> *I am God, and there is none like me."*   (Isaiah 46:9)

Babylon says,

> *"I am, and there is none besides me."*   (Isaiah 47:8)

Tyre says,

> *"I am a god;*
> *I sit on the throne of a god . . . "*   (Ezekiel 28:2)

■ *Idolatry, however, inevitably leads to demonization.* In discussing food offered to idols, Paul points out that the idols are nothing, but behind the idols there are demons receiving the worship (1 Corinthians 10:18–20). Thus, a corporate structure can be demonized in the same way as an individual.

■ *Nevertheless, the city, even in its fallenness is not to be rejected and not to be abandoned.* Firstly because it is the object of redemption, and secondly because restored and transformed, it is required for the service of God in the age to come.

The character of the city

The character of the fallen, rebellious city is analyzed with great accuracy and insight in Scripture. It is essential for us to understand it so that we know what we are up against in living in the city, and all its manifestations great and small.

We are not dealing here with flesh and blood, that is with the sins of people (Ephesians 6:12), but with the dimension of structural evil that works through people, fostering rampant greed, capitalizing on lust, inflaming violence and ruthlessly exploiting the weak and the helpless.

■ Because of its idolatrous drive, the city is not merely secular, and therefore religiously neutral, it is against God.

☐ It blasphemes God (Isaiah 37:23–24), defies Him (Jeremiah 50:29), and plots evil against Him (Nahum 1:11).

☐ It is full of idols, sorcery and witchcraft (Isaiah 47:9; Jeremiah 50:38; Nahum 3:4; Revelation 18:23).

☐ It is against the Church, the Lord's inheritance (Jeremiah 50:11).

■ Its chief aim is self-aggrandisement and it will use anything, including the Gospel and the Name of Christ to build up its status and position (Isaiah 13:10–11; 47:5; Jeremiah 51:41).
The drive of the city for greatness is manifested in:

☐ The accumulation of wealth (Ezekiel 28:4–5; Revelation 18:14–15).

☐ Architectural splendour and impressive constructions (Ezekiel 27; 3–12; Zechariah 9:3).

☐ A consumption economy, majoring on luxury and entertainment (Isaiah 23:7; Ezekiel 26:17; Revelation 18:3, 7).

☐ Self-confidence and an illusion of security (Zephaniah 2:15; Isaiah 47:8; Obadiah 3).

☐ Economic power, often based on dishonest trading, and exploitation of men and women (Isaiah 23:3–9; Amos 1:9; Ezekiel 27:12–23; 28:16–18).

☐ Expansion, conquest and colonization, seen in modern times in takeovers and multinational conglomorates (Isaiah 14:21; Jeremiah 50:23; Ezekiel 26:17).

☐ Wisdom and understanding put to corrupt purposes (Isaiah 47:10; Ezekiel 28:17).

■ The fallenness of the city further manifested in its characteristic forms of evil that include:

☐ Violence and cruelty (Nahum 3:1–3; Ezekiel 28:16).

☐ Arrogance and pride (Isaiah 10:12; Zechariah 10:11).

☐ Ruthlessness and aggression (Isaiah 14:4–6; Ezekiel 30:11; 32:12).

☐ Merciless oppression (Isaiah 14:17; 47:6).

☐ Dishonesty and injustice (Ezekiel 9:9; Nahum 3:1).

☐ Wickedness, evil standards (Jonah 1:1; Nahum 1:11; Isaiah 47:10).

☐ It destroys, devours and creates emptiness (Jeremiah 51:25, 35).

Understanding the structural powers

An understanding of the corporate spirit or personality helps to clarify some of the situations we commonly experience in the city. Here are some examples:

■ The sometimes rigid, implacable and irrational resistance to change in an organization of otherwise adaptable, reasonable and progressive individuals.

What we have come up against is the spirit of the organization that once set in its ways, is highly resistant to change.

■ The bitter power struggle that often takes place at an impalpable and suprahuman level in a business takeover, and why certain members of the management team of the business that has been captured are rapidly and ruthlessly dumped.

There is a life and death struggle between two cities and to the city, survival takes precedence over ethics, and the end will always justify the means. When one city wins, the people in the conquered city who are dropped, are not fired because of inefficiency but because they are not acceptable to, or don't "fit", the persona or spirit of the victorious city.

■ Why a church split is so devastating and so painful and leaves people hurt and scarred.

The corporate spirit, the "angel" of the church has been wounded and amputated.

■ Why a breakaway group formed by disgruntled, divisive people often becomes a bitter, divided church.

The persona that is created has the difficult characteristics of the founding flock.

■ Why the pervasiveness and seeming omnipotence of the city creates a feeling of helplessness amongst Christians and fosters a retreat from the secular city into the Christian "safe houses", that are the churches.

The skyline of the downtown area of the city is dominated by towering office blocks. They are the "high places". The gleaming skyscrapers are making a spiritual statement, "Here, we have the power! Here, we have the influence! Here, we command the resources! Here, you bow the knee to us!"

The Enemy in the Heavenlies

Under the dominion mandate, mankind had been given spiritual authority over the created world, that is:

☐ They were to represent the source of power in the world; that is God.

☐ They were to exercise the prerogatives of that power over creation in order to see that God's will was done on earth as it is in heaven.

☐ They were stewards; that is accountable to God for the way in which they fulfilled their role.

Because of the Fall, however, mankind lost access to the presence of God, therefore his authority over the world collapsed because it was no longer backed up by God's power. Into the spiritual vacuum that resulted, Satan came and usurped the place of authority. Now, opposed to the kingdom of God, there is a dominion of darkness (Colossians 1:13), a ruling system of demonic "powers" that dominate the structural "powers" of the world system and harden them in their rebellion against God.

If they are left to work unhindered these demonic powers will:

☐ Bring confusion and chaos into attempts to diagnose the real nature of the problems in society or to discover viable solutions to the problems.

☐ Seek to neutralize any potential threats to their control by spiritual or other attacks against anyone who represents a danger to that control.

☐ Frustrate attempts to reform the structural powers by hardening their resistance to change.

When we examine the nature of this domain of darkness we find a tightly knit hierarchy of evil powers. Here is a brief summary of the biblical evidence.

Satan

The dominion of darkness is under the direction and control of Satan, the fallen archangel. Two main passages describe his state and his fall (Isaiah 14:12–14 and Ezekiel 28:12–17).

■ In his unfallen state he was Lucifer, the morning star, son of the dawn. His realm was in heaven (Isaiah 14:12) and the Garden of Eden (Ezekiel 28:13).

■ Created blameless, he was the model of perfection, wisdom and beauty. He was a guardian cherub, that is with a particular role to do with the throne of God (Ezekiel 28:12–15).

■ Pride corrupted his wisdom (Ezekiel 28:17) and he aspired to the very throne of God, that is, to be equal with God.

> *"I will raise my throne*
> *above the stars* [angels] *of God;*

I will sit enthroned on the mount of assembly,
   on the utmost heights of the sacred mountain.
I will ascend above the tops of the clouds;
   I will make myself like the Most High."

(Isaiah 14:13–14)

■ In his unfallen state Satan was anointed, that is he had the Holy Spirit. When he sinned therefore, he sinned against the anointing, that is, his sin was the unpardonable sin against the Holy Spirit (Mark 3:29).

■ Because of his rebellion he was expelled in disgrace (Ekeziel 28:16) and cast down to earth (Isaiah 14:12; Luke 10:18).

■ Now Satan is Beelzebul ("Baal is prince") the prince or ruler (*archon*) of the demons (Matthew 12:24). He is also called the prince of this world (John 12:31; 14:30), and the god of this age (2 Corinthians 4:4). Moreover he is the *"prince of the power of the air, the spirit that is now at work in the sons of disobedience"* (Ephesians 2:2, RSV). Here the meaning is that he controls the spiritual atmosphere or climate of the fallen world.

■ As far as the Church is concerned, Satan is the enemy (1 Peter 5:8), the accuser or devil (Revelation 12:10; Ephesians 4:27), the deceiver and father of lies (2 Corinthians 11:13–14; John 8:44), and the tempter (1 Thessalonians 3:5).

■ His character is revealed in his names. Thus he is "the evil one" (Matthew 13:38; Ephesians 6:16; 1 John 5:19), Apollyon, "the destroyer" (Revelation 9:11), Belial, the spirit of worthlessness and emptiness (2 Corinthians 6:15), and murderer (John 8:44). The animal images used to describe him are those of serpent (Genesis 3:1ff.; 2 Corinthians 11:3), dragon (Revelation 12:9; 13:2; 20:2), and prowling lion (1 Peter 5:8).

■ Finally Satan's resources are described as including a throne or seat of power (Revelation 2:13; 16:10), strongholds (2 Corinthians 10:4), and secret ways of working (deep things), including the power to perform counterfeit miracles and signs (2 Thessalonians 2:7–9; Revelation 2:24).

A host of fallen angels

Satan is neither omnipotent, nor is he omnipresent, therefore he works through a host of fallen angels, perhaps one third of the heavenly hosts, who followed him in his rebellion (Revelation 12:4; 2 Peter 2:4). These beings are also called demons (Matthew 9:33–34; Luke 8:27ff.) and evil spirits or unclean spirits (Luke 8:29; Mark 9:25).

This army of evil spirit beings, organized in a hierarchy of demonic power structures dependent on the power of Satan, hold sway over the world system. They influence, manipulate and control the structural powers, confirming them in their rebellion against God, and using them as instruments of evil and oppression.

The shape of this structure is as follows:

■ *Geopolitical and geographic, or territorial powers*

☐ *World rulers (kosmoskrator*: Ephesians 6:12), *or rulers of this age.* These are the highest orders of powers directly under Satan himself, and the ones who clearly were involved in the most critical confrontation of all – engineering the death of Jesus (John 14:30; Luke 22:53; 1 Corinthians 2:6–8).

☐ *Principalities, princedoms or rulerships (archontes).* These are the powers over territories, perhaps the gods of the nations or the "sons of God", mentioned in Job 1:6 and 38:7.

> *"When the Most High gave to the nations their inheritance,*

> *when he separated the sons of men,*
> *he fixed the bounds of the peoples*
>   *according to the number of the sons of God."*
>
>   (Deuteronomy 32:8, RSV)

These angelic powers originally appointed to watch over the nations have apparently fallen after the fact of Satan's rebellion and have come under his influence (Psalm 82:1–2). They are referred to in Daniel 10:13, 20 as the *"prince of Persia"* and *"the prince of Greece"*.

☐ *Rulers (archon*: Colossians 1:16; Ephesians 1:21; 3:10; 6:12). These are perhaps the more numerous and lower orders, who are over specific regions, cities or territories.

■ *Powers over spheres of influence.* Another way of looking at these orders is to see their attachment as being to functional, rather than geographical areas of interest. We can distinguish what seems to be four distinct categories:

☐ *Dominions or lordships (kuriotes*: Colossians 1:16; Ephesians 1:21). These are demonic officers over particular cultural and social areas of influence. For example political, educational or philosophical ideologies or the media, the legal system or music, entertainment and the arts etc.

☐ *Powers (dunamis*: Romans 8:38; 1 Peter 3:22; Colossians 1:16). A multiplicity of controlling powers over specific institutions great and small – business corporations, educational establishments, welfare organizations, governing bodies, societies, clubs and associations of all kinds.

☐ *Authorities (exousia*: Colossians 2:15; Ephesians 3:10). Beings with the right, delegated to them from above, to exercise authority, that is to represent a power source and act on its behalf.

☐ *Spiritual forces (pneumatikos) of evil in the spiritual realm* (Ephesians 6:12). These relate particularly to activity in the realm of spirit such as false prophecy, false religions and heretical doctrine, occultism, witchcraft and the magic arts, and spurious miracles or deceiving signs (Jeremiah 14:14; Ezekiel 13:20–23; Acts 13:6; 1 John 4:1 etc.).

Christi and
the Powers

In spite of the Fall and the rebellion of mankind, God did not abandon His creation. The Incarnation is, in fact God's ultimate commitment to the work of His hands. The Son of God became part of the created order to redeem it back to its original purpose. The significance of this for the city, that is, the structural principalities and powers, is that we must not reject them, abandon them or withdraw from them because:

☐ In spite of the fallenness and rebellion of the structural powers, God maintains them in being, otherwise society would fall into chaos (Romans 13:1–6).

☐ The demonic powers are the object of divine judgment, but the structural powers are the object of redemption, that is to say, they are not only part of the *"all things"* of creation, in Colossians 1:16–17, they are also part of the *"all things"* of reconciliation in Colossians 1:20.

☐ Disarmed of their rebellion, and delivered from demonic control, the structural powers and their gifts are required for the age to come (1 Corinthians 15:24–28; Ephesians 1:10; Revelation 21:24–26).

We now have to see how the disarming and recovery of the powers has been effected.

The powers and first century Palestine

In Galatians 4:4 Paul, referring to the Incarnation, says, *"But when the time had fully come, God sent his Son..."* In other words, Jesus came into the world at a uniquely significant time in human history. But when we examine the Palestine of the first century into which He came, we come across a feature that has received very little attention – He came into a nation that was dominated by the principalities and powers:

■ *Palestine was under the heel of a strong military power*, the Roman Empire. It was an occupied country, there were foreign troops in complete control of the nation.

■ *It was under a legalistic religious power*, the synagogue and the Sanhedrin, so intolerant that they tried to assassinate Jesus just because He healed the sick on the Sabbath day.

■ *The nation was crushed by the harsh, oppressive, economic and civil power* of the Herodians who farmed out the taxes and kept most of the population in abject poverty, to finance their grandiose life style and building projects.

■ *More ominous still, the country was under demonic power* to an unusual extent. When you read the Old Testament you find very few references to evil spirits and very few examples of demonized people, apart from spirit mediums, astrologers and diviners. But when you turn to the Gospels, they are everywhere, and the casting out of demons was a dramatic part of Jesus' public ministry. The evidence seems to indicate a massive eruption of demons into the nation, as though Satan was expecting an attack on his domain and was preparing against it.

Jesus and the powers

In His Incarnate humanity Jesus lived a life of perfect freedom under the powers. The powers could do nothing with Him. None of us are free, the way Jesus was free. We can be managed by one of two traits, one is greed and the other is fear, the carrot or the stick. The powers are confident that every man has his price and every man has his breaking point.

But what do you do with a man like Jesus? He had no greed whatsoever.

> *"Foxes have holes and birds of the air have nests, but the Son of Man has nowhere to lay his head."*   (Matthew 8:20)

Yet He could have had everything He wanted. When the devil offered Him the kingdoms of the world in return for His worship, that was nonsense. Jesus could have taken the world over any time He chose, and not by any divine power, but by the sheer moral force of one single perfectly whole and perfectly uncorrupted human will. We have no conception of the moral energy He could have generated had He wanted to. No one could have resisted Him. He could have walked into the senate in Rome and said to Caesar, "Get down off that throne. I have taken the world over." But Jesus did not do that, He was after something much greater. He had come to end the sin problem for ever, and that required a Cross.

Furthermore Jesus had no fear. In the boat with the disciples in a demon inspired storm that left them irrational with terror, His response when wakened from sleep was *"Why are you so afraid?"* (Matthew 8:26). What do you do with a man who has no greed and no fear? You can't do anything.

■ Jesus demonstrated His freedom from the power of the synagogue by healing on the Sabbath day. We read that He travelled throughout Galilee, preaching in their synagogues, healing the sick and driving out demons (Matthew 4:23; Mark 1:39). If He did it in the synagogues it would always be on the Sabbath. Why did Jesus deliberately and consistently perform miracles on the Sabbath day (Matthew 9:35; 12:9–13; Mark 6:1–4; Luke 13:10–16; 14:1–4; John 5:6–10; 9:1–16)? He was refusing to submit to the spirit of the synagogue.

■ Some Pharisees came to Jesus one time and warned Him to hide because Herod wanted to kill Him. Jesus' reply? *"Go tell that fox, 'I will drive out demons and heal people today and tomorrow, and on the third day I will reach my goal'"* (Luke 13:32). He refused to submit to the economic/civil power of the house of Herod.

■ When Jesus appears before Pilate, the Roman said, *"Don't you realise I have power either to free you or to crucify you?"* Jesus' reply showed who was master, *"You would have no power over me if it were not given to you from above"* (John 19:10–11). No wonder it was Pilate who was afraid.

■ Even more dramatically, Jesus faces the strong man, Satan himself (Matthew 4:1–11). There in the most unfavorable of conditions, not in a garden like Eden but in the wilderness, not freshly rested but after forty days of fasting, He met all the subtlety and power of the fallen archangel, not in one temptation but in three, and came off victorious. Jesus faced Satan, eyeball to eyeball, as the Spirit-filled Man, and established once for all His moral ascendancy over the devil. Henceforth in His ministry He drives out the demons with a word; having bound the strong man He proceeds to plunder His house (Matthew 12:25–29).

Jesus taught His disciples the same freedoms – not to be afraid of the power of the synagogue and the ruling authorities

(Luke 12:4–11), not to be afraid of the power of possessions and economic survival (Matthew 6:25–35), and not to be afraid of the power of Satan (Luke 10:18–20).

The surrender to the powers

Then at the end of Jesus' three years of ministry we come to the amazing paradox – **Jesus surrenders to the powers**. The religious power arrests Him without resistance, interrogates Him, tries Him before the Sanhedrin for blasphemy, and hands Him over to the military power. The military power tries to palm the problem off on to the civil power and send Him to Herod, then when He is sent back, it brutally flogs Him and then crucifies Him. The economic power strips Him stark naked on the Cross and gambles His clothes away.

But there was something even stranger – Jesus surrenders to the satanic power. He said, *"This is your hour, and the power of darkness"* (Luke 22:53, RSV). When the sky was darkened as Jesus hung on the Cross, it was not nature hiding its face from the sight, it was the hour and power of darkness. There was one hour in all eternity, one place in the whole universe, when Satan must have thought he had everything in his grasp. He had the *Logos*, the eternal Son of God, a willing helpless victim in his hands, and he crucified Him.

The victory of the Cross

The Cross was Satan's undoing, he never realized until too late what would happen on the Cross, for even in His dying Jesus preserved His freedom, His life was not taken from Him, He yielded it up (Luke 23:46).

In 1 Corinthians chapter 2 Paul is dealing with the secret wisdom of God revealed in the Cross, and then he makes this statement:

> *"None of the rulers of this age understood it, for if they had,*
> *they would not have crucified the Lord of glory."*
>
> (1 Corinthians 2:8)

The rulers of this age are the demonic world rulers who engineered the death of Jesus. What Paul is saying is that if Satan had had any idea of what was going to happen through the Cross, he would have levelled every tree in Palestine rather than let them use one to crucify Jesus!

What was the wisdom of the Cross?

■ Jesus' death on our behalf, cancelled the destructive power of sin and the punishment of the law that was against us.

> *"When you were dead in your sins and in the uncircumcision of*
> *your sinful nature, God made you alive with Christ. He forgave*
> *us all our sins, having cancelled the written code, with its regu-*
> *lations, that was against us and that stood opposed to us; he*
> *took it away, nailing it to the cross."*   (Colossians 2:13–14)

■ By His death and resurrection Jesus robbed Satan of his strongest weapon against us, the power of death, and thus effectively disarmed him.

> *"Since the children have flesh and blood, he too shared in their*
> *humanity so that by his death he might destroy him who holds*
> *the power of death – that is, the devil – and free those who all*
> *their lives were held in slavery by their fear of death."*
>
> (Hebrews 2:14–15)

The word "destroy" is the Greek *katargeo*, literally "to reduce to inactivity", thus "abolish, disarm, render powerless or nullify".

■ He also disarmed the principalities and powers.

> *"And having disarmed the powers and authorities, he made a*
> *public spectacle of them, triumphing over them by the cross."*
> (Colossians 2:15)

The image here is of the Roman triumph when the defeated
foes were led in a public parade behind the victor. In this sense
the powers have been exposed, stripped, disarmed and un-
masked by the death and resurrection of Jesus.

Which powers have been disarmed?

The question then arises, which powers have been disarmed,
the structural powers, represented by the city, or the demonic
powers represented by the watching angel behind the city?

The answer is – both! Jesus has established His authority
over both the demonic and the structural powers, so that He
could say,

> *"All authority in heaven and on earth* [eternal and temporal,
> spiritual and secular] *has been given to me."*
> (Matthew 28:18)

The significance of this is momentous:

■ It means that there is authority in the Name of Jesus to
enable us to bind the demonic powers in the spiritual realm
and cast them out of the structures, thus opening the structures
up to change.

■ It also means that we can challenge the rebelliousness of
the structural powers with the claims of the Lordship of Jesus
Christ and in the long run they have to yield. That is what
makes real cultural change possible.

"...Jesus Christ, who has gone into heaven and is at God's right hand – with angels, authorities and powers in submission to him."   (1 Peter 3:21–22)

The source of the victory of the Cross

We still have to ask – what was in the death of Jesus on the Cross that so thoroughly defeated the powers? It was not His death as death that accomplished the victory, nor was it His surrender to the powers. Evil is not overcome by mere surrender to its wickedness as though it will finally be sated by being given a free hand to indulge itself to the utmost.

The power that was in the death of Jesus was that it was death in obedience.

"He ...
became obedient to death – even death on a cross!"
                                        (Philippians 2:8).

What drives the principalities and powers is the energy of rebellion against God. Jesus faced that rebellion with ultimate obedience to the Father's will. All the efforts of the powers were directed to one end, to stir in the human heart of Jesus a flicker of resistance to the Father's will, a flicker of self-preservation and resistance to the destiny chosen for Him. Their treatment of Jesus can be explained from no other source – the hours of interrogation, the sadistic brutal torture and mockery of a man doomed to die, the taunts to come down from the Cross.

But they failed. Jesus met them all with obedience, obedience, obedience, until finally the powers could go no further. His ultimate obedience exhausted the rebellion of the powers until they fell back defeated, debilitated, neutralized and depotentiated. In the end even death had to yield and Jesus rose triumphant over death and Hades.

Now He reigns, and will reign until all the structural powers have been purged of their rebellion and acknowledge His Lordship.

Redemption Restores Creation

In the previous chapter we saw something of the triumph of the Cross over the principalities and powers, both structural and demonic. Now we need to examine what that means for the powers themselves.

God's purpose in redemption was twofold:

1. To restore all creation, with man as its steward, to its original state, under the headship of Christ.

    "With a view to an administration suitable to the fullness of the times, that is, the summing up of all things in Christ, things in the heavens and things on the earth."

    (Ephesians 1:10, NASB)

2. Not only to restore creation to its original state but to transform it as the arena for the display of the Father's glory in the age to come.

    ". . . the creation itself will be liberated from its bondage to decay and brought into the glorious freedom of the children of God." (Romans 8:21)

    "For the earth will be filled with the knowledge of the glory of the LORD, as the waters cover the sea." (Habakkuk 2:14)

All the great words of salvation have this common theme of restoring something back to its original state or purpose.

☐ **Redemption** is bringing back into freedom those who have gone into slavery.

☐ **Regeneration** is giving life back to something that has died.

☐ **Reconciliation** is bringing back into harmony those who are at odds with one another.

☐ **Restoration** is recovering a former state that has been lost. Even salvation has the sense of salvaging or bringing back to safety something that is in peril or danger.

How far does redemption reach?

The answer to the question as to how far redemption reaches, is that redemption recovers all that sin has lost. The Blood reaches as far as sin has gone, and sin has ruined, not just mankind, but the whole created order.

> *"We know that the whole creation has been groaning as in the pains of childbirth right up to the present time."*
>
> (Romans 8:22)

The intractable problems of society are not merely the sinfulness of fallen men. There is structural evil, an evil in the systems. All the structures of society, the city, the principalities and powers are also sin-damaged.

But if sin has penetrated the fabric of society, so does the Blood of Christ – *"where sin increased, grace increased all the more"* (Romans 5:20). The Church insists, and rightly so, that salvation is not just a personal matter, it must radically affect my marriage and family relationships. But marriage and family are only one of a whole network of relationships that make up life. Why draw the limit for redemption around the family? Why not my work, my community life or my political affiliation?

There is in fact, no biblical warrant for excluding any of these areas, in fact the reverse. The land is included, and the restoration of the city is included.

> *"If my people, who are called by my name, will humble themselves and pray and seek my face and turn from their wicked ways, then will I hear from heaven and will forgive their sin and will heal their land."*   (2 Chronicles 7:14)

Isaiah 61 is the passage that Jesus read out in the synagogue in Nazareth.

> *"The Spirit of the Lord GOD is upon me,*
> *Because the LORD has anointed me*
> *To bring good news to the afflicted;*
> *He has sent me to bind up the brokenhearted,*
> *To proclaim liberty to captives*
> *And freedom to prisoners;*
> *To proclaim the favorable year of the LORD."*
> (Isaiah 61:1–2, NASB)

Jesus stopped there for His purposes. We go on to apply the next verses to much of what has happened in the charismatic renewal:

> *"To comfort all who mourn,*
> *To grant those who mourn in Zion,*
> *Giving them a garland instead of ashes,*
> *The oil of gladness instead of mourning,*
> *The mantle of praise instead of a spirit of fainting.*
> *So they will be called oaks of righteousness,*
> *The planting of the LORD, that He may be glorified."*
> (Isaiah 61:2–3, NASB)

We stop there, but the prophecy does not stop there, it says *"Then . . . "*, that is after all the foregoing has happened:

> *"Then they will rebuild the ancient ruins,*
> *They will raise up the former devastations;*
> *And they will repair the ruined cities,*
> *The desolations of many generations.*
> *Strangers will stand and pasture your flocks,*
> *And foreigners will be your farmers and your vinedressers.*
> *But you will be called the priests of the* LORD*;*
> *You will be spoken of as ministers of our God."*
>
> (Isaiah 61:4–6, NASB)

The message is clear. When we receive the oil of joy and the mantle of praise we will be called the planting of the Lord.

But when we rebuild the ruined cities, then we will be called the priests of the Lord and the ministers of our God.

Deliverance and blessing

There are two dominant biblical themes of salvation:

1. ***Salvation as deliverance***. Christ has *"delivered us out of the power of darkness"* (Colossians 1:13 ASB) and from the devil (Hebrews 2:14). God will deliver us from all our troubles (Psalm 34:19), and from all our enemies (Psalm 18:16–19).

2. ***Salvation as blessing***. Christ brings us the blessing of eternal life (Ephesians 2:5), of forgiveness (Colossians 1:14), sanctification (1 Peter 1:2), healing (Acts 10:38), sonship (Galatians 4:5), and inheritance (Ephesians 1:14).

Salvation for the city involves both deliverance and blessing.

■ *The demonic principalities over the city have to be overthrown*. They are the object of judgment, not the object of redemption. We have to learn, not only how to drive demons out of people, but how to drive demons out of structures, so that the structural powers can be recovered. That is the realm of strategic (Level 3), spiritual warfare that we will deal with in chapter 8.

■ *The structural powers have to be reclaimed* because they are the objects of redemption, not destruction. That will involve:

☐ Spiritual warfare to quell their rebellion and unrighteous activities and to overthrow their idolatrous claims.

☐ Challenging them with the Lordship of Christ and calling them back to fulfill their rightful destiny as servants of Jesus Christ. This is the realm of redemptive organizational change that we will deal with in chapter 7.

The final future of the powers

Our present response towards the city, and the powers the city symbolizes, will depend a great deal on what our perspective is for their future. There is little incentive to spend time and effort on a lost cause.

Thankfully the powers are not a lost cause. Because they are part of the "all things" of creation (Colossians 1:16), their destruction or annihilation in the consummation of all things (Ephesians 1:10) would mark, not a victory for God but a defeat. But they are, as we have seen already, part of the "all things" of reconciliation, and are required for the age to come when we find them subject to the true Head, Jesus Christ, who is seated at God's right hand in the heavenly realms,

*"far above all rule and authority, power and dominion, and
every title that can be given, not only in the present age but also
in the one to come."*   (Ephesians 1:21)

At present we live in the tension between the Kingdom of
God that is both here, and not yet here; present in principle,
but not yet present in fullness.

When we examine God's redemptive work in the individual and His redemptive work in the city, we will find that
they parallel each other. In each case there are two distinct
stages, that can be described as:

1. God's continuous work, and

2. God's discontinuous work.

In the individual

■ *God's continuous work is the work of sanctification.* In
this we are being progressively changed by the Holy Spirit
to become in character more and more like Jesus Christ
(Romans 8:29; 2 Corinthians 3:18). This will go on all our
lives.

■ *God's discontinuous work is the work of glorification.* It
occurs when we die, or when Jesus returns, and is a dramatic,
instantaneous, radical change that is no more continuance of
the work of sanctification. In a moment, in the twinkling of
an eye, we will be changed, mortal will be clothed with
immortality, the natural body will become a spiritual body
of power and glory, and we will be like Jesus because
we will see him as he is (1 John 3:2; 1 Corinthians 15:42–
44, 52–54; 2 Corinthians 5:4; Philippians 3:21). We can read
the words but what they are trying to convey is almost
unimaginable.

In the principalities and powers

■ *God's continuous work in the city is the work of restoration.* The city rebels, the city is destroyed, the city repents, like Nineveh (Jonah 3:1–10) and the city is rebuilt, like Jerusalem (Nehemiah 2:5–6:15).

■ *God's discontinuous work is the work of transformation.* In the end the transformed city, the New Jerusalem comes down from God out of heaven (Revelation 21:2–27). It is a city of unimaginable beauty and splendour, and,

> *"The nations will walk by its light, and the kings of the earth will bring their splendour into it. On no day will its gates ever be shut, for there will be no night there. The glory and honour of the nations will be brought into it."*
>
> (Revelation 21:24–26)

What is to be our present response?

Here we tend to come up against competing eschatologies. One scenario says in effect that the powers (the city) is either beyond redemption or is merely to be testified against, or its recovery is none of our business because Christ is going to do it all at His Second Coming. That would be like saying that our ongoing struggle against personal sin and failure is hopeless, or it is unnecessary because we are all going to be perfect anyway when Jesus comes. No-one could find warrant for that view in Scripture.

The other scenario says that it is our responsibility to Christianize the whole world and the whole institutional structure of society before it is possible for Jesus to come back and reign.

That is like saying we will gradually become more and more holy and more and more perfect until one day we are too good for this earth and Jesus will have to take us into heaven.

The truth lies between these extremes.

It is evident from Scripture and experience that it is possible, before Jesus comes back, to have redeemed individuals who are not yet perfect, but who are radically changed from what they were before.

In the same way, it is possible, before Jesus returns, to have redeemed but not perfect business organizations, redeemed but not perfect economic systems and educational institutions, redeemed but not perfect cities and redeemed but not perfect nations.

It is to the practical implications of these truths that we now turn.

Living with Principalities and Powers

6

How then, as Christians, are we meant to live amongst the structural powers? For live in them we must in one manifestation or other. A useful way to approach the question is to go back to the three levels mentioned in chapter 1:

☐ Level 1: The individual or personal level

☐ Level 2: The suprahuman or structural level

☐ Level 3: The supernatural or demonic level

The individual and the powers

This is the most common level at which we experience the reality of the principalities and powers. We meet them in businesses, at school, in hospitals or government offices, in clubs and in the local church. We are involved with them in every area of our life. Here are the important points to remember:

■ Regardless of the fallenness of the powers we can live and work in them and, like Daniel or Joseph, serve their legitimate ends and rise to positions of authority and influence in them.

In doing so, moreover, we are to serve wholeheartedly, as if we are serving the Lord, not men (Ephesians 6:5–7) and we are to give everyone their due, whether it is taxes, or payment or respect or honor (Romans 13:7).

■ But while we live in the powers and serve their ends, we also live under the Lordship of Christ and that guarantees our moral freedom. Therefore we are not to yield to the idolatrous spirit of the powers, but to walk in faith and obedience like Shadrach, Meshach and Abednego (Daniel 3:1ff.) and like Daniel himself (Daniel 6:1ff.). That means:

☐ We are not to take our moral standards or our value system from the principalities and powers, or allow them to water down our Christian values so that they conform to the mind-set of the world. Read again the biblical character analysis of the city (chapter 2) and you will see why we need to have our minds continually renewed by the Holy Spirit and the Word of God (Romans 12:2).

☐ We must never allow the powers to become the ultimate authority in our lives as they will always try to do. In fact if you yield to the spirit of an organization, you can break all its rules and it will still look after you. If you refuse to yield to the corporate spirit, you may keep all its rules but it will try to get rid of you or try to destroy you. Only our willing submission to the Lordship of Christ guarantees our freedom against the powers. If we bow to Christ we need not bow to Caesar.

☐ We must reckon realistically with the fact that from time to time we will also come under spiritual attack from demonic principalities and powers. Remember that the attack will most often come through people, but people are never the enemy. It often takes real discernment to identify the true source of the attack (Matthew 16:21–23). Furthermore, we need to understand the principles of defensive warfare so that we can maintain our ground.

Defensive spiritual warfare

This is explained in more detail in Section 3.

The situations in which we are likely to come under spiritual attack from demonic principalities and powers could be one of the following:

■ We are threatening the enemy's possessions or position. Even a lone Christian standing simply in the Lordship of Jesus is posing an awesome threat to the fancied omnipotence of the powers, both structural and demonic.

■ The enemy is probing for our weaknesses, because Satan believes that we all have our price and our areas of vulnerability.

■ The enemy is trying to disable our defenses, isolate us from God and from other believers, and if possible seduce us or destroy us.

The principles of defensive warfare

Here are the main principles we must master to overcome in situations where the enemy is attacking us.

1. Occupy the high ground

The high ground is the ground where we have access to power, knowledge and defensive resources. Notice David's reliance on the spiritual high ground of God's presence (Psalms 18:2–3, 16–19; 27:5; 61:2–3 etc.). Our high ground is:

■ *Our revelation standing or position in Christ.*

> *"God raised us up with Christ and seated us with him in the*
> *heavenly realms in Christ Jesus."*   (Ephesians 2:6)
> (See also Ephesians 1:18–23; Colossians 3:1–4.)

■ *The victory of the cross and resurrection of Christ.* In the
New Testament this is sometimes summarized as "the blood
of the Lamb" (Colossians 2:15; Hebrews 2:14; Revelation
12:11).

■ *Our position in the Body of Christ and in the covenantal*
relationships belonging to it (Ephesians 4:10–16).

Satan will always try to draw us off our high ground and on
to his ground by deception or by capitalizing on areas of
ignorance, or by tempting us to rebellion.

2. Build an effective defense system
This is all-important. Our defense system must be in place
before it is needed and must become familiar to us and effective
through practice. Note the following important aspects:

■ *Develop an attitude of confidence* (Psalm 27:3; Jeremiah
17:7). Deal with fear. Fear destroys morale (Deuteronomy
20:8) and tends to produce the very thing we are afraid of (Job
3:25). The answer to fear is, like Elisha's servant, to see the
true reality of the situation we face:

> *"Those who are with us are more than those who are with*
> *them."*   (2 Kings 6:16)

Or like Paul:

> *"If God is for us, who can be against us?"*   (Romans 8:31)

■ *Clear away entanglements that inhibit our effectiveness and render us vulnerable.* These may include relational entanglements (2 Corinthians 6:14), financial entanglements (1 Timothy 6:9–10), debilitating habits or thought patterns that drain our energy (Matthew 6:25–34; 1 Corinthians 9:25–27), non-productive activities that merely complicate things and issues, or circumstances that are not really our responsibility (Hebrews 12:1).

■ *Understand the importance of the armor of God.* The armor of God is a set of life conditions that God wants to establish in our lives, that enable Him to work and prevent Satan from working. But we have to "put on" the armor, that is to say, life conditions only work if we make them ours; they cannot be imposed on us or imparted to us without our deliberate appropriation.

There are many life conditions that are important in our Christian life but it seems that the following ones are vital in terms of spiritual warfare:

☐ *Truth* (Ephesians 6:14; 2 Corinthians 6:7). The effect of truth is to expose untruth and therefore protect us from the devil's lies and deception (John 3:19–21).

☐ *Righteousness.* Our covenant relationship with God through Christ, that guarantees our safety and ensures victory (Ephesians 6:14; 2 Corinthians 6:7; Isaiah 59:17).

☐ *Peace* (Ephesians 6:15; Romans 16:20). Not only peace with God but the peace of God to guard or garrison our hearts and minds (Philippians 4:7; Colossians 3:15).

☐ *Faith* (Ephesians 6:16; 1 Thessalonians 5:8). Faith is the creative link that enables God's power to be shared with man (1 John 5:4).

☐ *Hope* (Ephesians 6:17; 1 Thessalonians 5:8). Hope is the confident expectation of something good, in other words the openness that enables us to receive.

☐ *Love* (1 Thessalonians 5:8; 2 Corinthians 6:6). Love not only links us to the life of God, but is the life of God and overcomes the world (1 John 5:2–5).

☐ *The word of God* (Ephesians 6:17). This is the *rhema*, the Spirit-quickened revelatory word with which Jesus overcame Satan, with which He sustains all things in being (Hebrews 1:3). It is of eternal relevance and effectiveness, *"the word* [rhema] *of the Lord stands forever"* (1 Peter 1:25).

☐ *Prayer in the Spirit* (Ephesians 6:18; Jude 20). Important for building up or strengthening the human spirit.

■ *Examine your resources.* Assess your personal life and experience to discover:

☐ Your spiritual strengths, the things you know and the things you do well. These are things you need to build on.

☐ Your weaknesses and vulnerabilities. These are things for which you may need to devise protective strategies.

☐ Your relationships, those people you can depend on for support in difficult times and with whom you can work effectively.

■ *Learn to handle spiritual pressure.* Under pressure or attack we revert to our deepest responses – the things we truly know and the things we can trust in any and every circumstance. But spiritual attack or pressure rarely sends any advance warning so we need to know:

☐ The nature of the truth that constitutes our secure ground.

☐ How to fall back instinctively and automatically on to that strong place, so that it is a well practiced manoeuvre.

3. Learn from the experiences

We want to do more than just survive attacks or successfully defend our position. We can learn useful lessons from them if we pay attention:

■ We can discover our weaknesses that cause us to sin and experience grace to overcome next time.

■ We can find out Satan's views as to where our vulnerabilities lie and can develop protective strategies to counter such attacks.

■ We can experience God's interventions on our behalf and build our faith and confidence for the future (2 Corinthians 1:10).

■ We can learn the spiritual skills of interdependence within the Body of Christ, where we stand together against the enemy (Ephesians 6:19).

Redeeming the Structural Powers

7

Living and working in the powers but keeping ourselves free from their pressure to conform is important, but even more important is recovering them to their rightful role as servants of Jesus Christ the Lord. That is rebuilding the ruined cities.

Remember always that we are dealing with two different dimensions of the problem:

1. Spiritual warfare against the demonic powers behind the structures. The structural powers will resist change in any event, but the demonic powers will, unless they are dealt with, reinforce that resistance, and wear out those who attempt to alter the status quo.

2. Influence and redemptive organizational change in the structural powers. The two must go hand in hand for if we do not become actively engaged in working for organizational change, all our spiritual warfare will be unproductive, or even counterproductive as Jesus warned in Matthew 12:43–45. What is usually overlooked in this passage is that Jesus applied the analogy of the re-demonized individual to describe the state of an entire society.

Identifying the character of the powers

Our first task is to identify the corporate culture or inner spirit of the city, so that we understand that character of the power we are seeking to influence. That involves observation and inquiry, specifically into the following areas.

1. The physical environment

The state of buildings, facilities and the physical surroundings says a good deal about the character of the power, just as the state of a house tells you a lot about the occupants. For example, are they dirty, neglected and run-down, or bright, clean and modern; a stark, sterile, concrete jungle; a make-shift, second-hand jumble, or a tasteful, conservative, decor?

2. What the city says about itself

This is the self-image of the city. It can be discovered from:

☐ Reports, press releases, advertisements and pronouncements by public officials, etc.

☐ Its origins and recorded history.

☐ More important, the unofficial history and its popular myths, anecdotes and legends.

3. How it greets strangers

☐ How the "in" group is distinguished from the "out" group.

☐ How those "inside" talk about or treat "outsiders". Are they welcomed or ignored, appreciated or resented, treated as visitors or intruders, looked up to or looked down on, etc.?

4. The shared values

Shared values are the basic concepts and beliefs widely held and endorsed by the organization. These may not be at all what they are officially said to be, but they can be inferred from:

☐ The activities people spend most of their time and energy on.

☐ The things that are regarded as the keys to success or acceptance.

☐ The things that get the most public attention – media publicity, advertising budgets etc.

☐ The things that people talk about most or that create the greatest controversy – opinion pools, talk-back shows, letters to the press etc.

☐ The things that draw the biggest crowds.

5. The heroes

Heroes are individuals who personify the shared values of the culture. They are found amongst:

☐ Those who are prominent in the public eye as making success seem attainable.

☐ Those who provide role-models for others to follow, emulate or aspire to be like.

☐ Those who set the fashions in dress, behavior or lifestyle.

☐ Historical figures and the stories, myths and legends that accumulate around them.

6. The rituals

Rituals are expressive events that help to underscore and communicate the shared values of the culture, for example:

☐ Social rituals that show how to get into the culture, or what social standards are acceptable in it.

☐ Recognition rituals, that is, how success or achievement is recognized or rewarded.

☐ Extravaganzas, such as celebrations, commemorations or festivals.

Organizational change agent – Nehemiah

A detailed biblical blueprint for organizational change can be found in the book of Nehemiah. It has particular relevance to our present study because it deals with the rebuilding of the city. The temple had been rebuilt by Ezra seventy years before but the city was still in ruins. The last thirty years of the charismatic renewal has seen a substantial rebuilding of the Church, but our society, the city, is in ruins.

Here is a summary of Nehemiah's method. It has widespread application to the "cities" in which we live and work today.

1. Care for the city

When Nehemiah heard of the state of Jerusalem he *"sat down and wept and mourned for days"* (Nehemiah 1:4, NASB). John Greenleaf says that the problem with our society is that nobody loves the institutions. We fear and dislike the structural powers, we are overawed and repelled by them, we submit to them and are sometimes bought and seduced by them, but we do not care for them. Care is nothing less than love in action and if we are ever going to change the city we need to care for it the way a Jew cared for Jerusalem.

"If I forget you, O Jerusalem,
may my right hand forget its skill.
May my tongue cling to the roof of my mouth
if I do not remember you,
If I do not consider Jerusalem
my highest joy." (Psalm 137:5–6)

2. Pray for the city

"For some days I mourned and fasted and prayed before the God of heaven..." (see Nehemiah 1:4–11). Nehemiah's prayer contains two valuable insights for organizational change agents:

■ He identified himself with the sin of the city. *"...confess the sins we Israelites, including myself and my father's house, have committed against you"* (Nehemiah 1:6). The city is a corporate entity with corporate evil and because we are a part of its corporate existence we share a real corporate responsibility for its wrongdoing.

■ He was willing to become part of the answer to his own prayer (Nehemiah 1:11). Genuine intercession very often leads to intervention but genuine intercession also requires of the intercessor the willingness to be the one who undertakes the intervention.

3. Plan for the city

A period of about four months elapsed between the events of chapter 1 and those of chapter 2 of Nehemiah when Nehemiah appeared before the king and queen. What he asked for then was not the result of instant inspiration but the fruit of weeks of prayer and careful deliberation. What came out of that preparation was:

■ *A big vision*. What 50,000 Jews under Zerubbabel had failed to accomplish in seventy years, Nehemiah decided he would do. He said, *"I can rebuild it"* (Nehemiah 2:5). When it comes to changing a power or rebuilding a city, great or small, we will accomplish nothing without a vision that is big enough to go for radical and not mere cosmetic change.

■ *A long-term goal.* The king asked Nehemiah how long he would be away and Nehemiah *"set a time"* (Nehemiah 2:6). Compare Nehemiah 2:1 and Nehemiah 13:6 and you find the time was twelve years! Institutional change takes time and the more radical the changes the longer it will take. Therefore to succeed we have to be committed for the long haul.

4. Live in the city
With a true instinct for what was involved Nehemiah came and lived in the city (Nehemiah 2:11). We will never change an institution unless we get "in" because change can only come from within. Getting in will require a respectful, non-judgmental and humble willingness to learn the ways of the city and share in its life.

5. Know the city
By the time Nehemiah had been in the city for less than a week he knew its state and its problems as well as anyone:

☐ He saw its problems with the objectivity and fresh eyes of a newcomer not conditioned by the culture to accept its ways;

☐ He examined the situation personally and at first hand so he could make up his mind without the excuses and rationalizations of the inhabitants, and most important of all;

☐ He saw the problems from the perspective of someone who believed they could be overcome and who intended to do something about it.

6. Start a movement

Radical change in a culture or the life of an organization is always accomplished by a "movement" which has the specific aim of bringing about the desired changes. A movement does not require a majority before it can be launched. It can be initiated by a small dedicated minority, but once launched it can gain a momentum of its own. What Nehemiah did was to initiate just such a movement. Here is his strategy which can be applied to small and large scale organizations alike:

■ Find the influencers (Nehemiah 2:16), the key people whose views count and who set the trends other people follow.

■ Get them to face the problem (Nehemiah 2:17), but note that Nehemiah made their problem his too. He said, *"You see the trouble we are in."* He did not say, "See the trouble you are in." The identification of the change agent with the problem is all important.

■ Give them a vision (Nehemiah 2:17). *"Come, let us rebuild the wall of Jerusalem and we will no longer be in disgrace."* But note that Nehemiah was not just talking vision, he had already made some of the critical decisions that would make it possible to actualize the vision (Nehemiah 2:17–18).

■ Get them to buy into the vision for themselves. *"They replied 'Let us start rebuilding'"* (Nehemiah 2:18). This is the critical point in any movement for change, it has to be owned by those who will run with it, so that it is no longer the vision of the change agent, it is the vision of the movement.

7. Foster the growth of the movement for change

These are the characteristics that need to be identified and then fostered or encouraged:

■ Personal commitment by individuals who believe they can change their immediate environment.

■ Recruitment of friends and colleagues to join in small-scale efforts, or "winnable opportunities" for change. The successful movements accumulate a track record of small but observable success in changing things until gradually they accumulate growing support (see Nehemiah 3).

■ Expectation of, and willingness to face opposition from the establishment. When a movement is under way, opposition and attack only strengthens its resolve (Nehemiah 2:20; 4:1ff.).

■ The willingness to go for radical and fundamental rather than peripheral change and the ability to discern the difference. Nehemiah faced the threat of violent opposition but also the more subtle distraction of a negotiated settlement (Nehemiah 6:1–9).

8. Reiterate, reinforce and restate the goals as required along the way

Even when change is under way the work is not finished:

■ The vision has to be repeated and expressed in ways that are appropriate to each stage of the movement's development.

■ People have to be continually encouraged, motivated, corrected and sometimes disciplined along the way (Nehemiah 4:14; 5:1–13).

■ Difficulties have to be faced, problems solved and the movement represented to the outside world (Nehemiah 4:16–20).

9. Finally...

Along with and even after radical change, there is the on-going process of re-educating and re-ordering the inner life of the city.

The first six chapters of Nehemiah deal with the rebuilding of the walls of the city, the next six chapters deal with the even more difficult task of reforming its character. The last chapter is a timely warning that the task is never complete in this age, and the possibility of backsliding into the old ways is an ever-present possibility.

Strategic Level Spiritual Warfare

Dealing with the strong man

We come now to probably the most serious level of the conflict: strategic level spiritual warfare against demonic principalities and powers that dominate and manipulate the structural powers. Their influence is seen at all levels and just as readily in boardrooms and council chambers, with the confusing of ethical issues, the blatant amorality of some decisions and the overall sense of something vastly wise operating behind the scenes and manipulating the puppets.

Dealing with these powers is a matter of first order of importance otherwise our efforts to recover the structural powers for the Kingdom are doomed to failure. Jesus emphasized this when he said,

> *"Or how can anyone enter the strong man's house and carry off his property, unless he first binds the strong man? And then he will plunder his house."* (Matthew 12:29, NASB)

While Satan is the strong man, there will generally be in any specific territory or functional area in which an organization operates, a "strong man" who represents the power source and the dominating influence in that particular area.

To attempt to change the attitude and culture of a city or a single organization before the demonic powers are dealt with, is like trying to rob a strong man's house while the strong man is still there and unhampered in his activity.

> *"When a strong man, fully armed, guards his own house, his possessions are safe. But when someone stronger attacks and overpowers him, he takes away the armour in which the man trusted and divides up the spoils."*   (Luke 11:21–22)

This is the realm of offensive spiritual warfare. It is not the place for rash, impetuous and ill-conceived forays by enthusiastic raw recruits and needs to be treated with the seriousness with which it is dealt in Scripture.

Offensive spiritual warfare

It must be emphasized again that what we are dealing with is neither imaginary or metaphorical war, it is real spiritual war with real enemies, real spiritual bullets and sadly, real casualties. At the same time our objective is always total victory, and the complete confusion and defeat of the enemy (Exodus 17:13–14). Defeat is a shame and dishonor (2 Kings 19:3), there are no points for a "good show" or a good loser.

It is also important to understand that spiritual warfare is necessary for our full development. Thus we should not be surprised to discover that to Israel, peace (*shalom*) did not mean the absence of war, it meant:

☐ Complete harmony and unity among friends, and

☐ Complete victory in the war against enemies.

That is why Paul could write to the Romans *"The God of peace will soon crush Satan under your feet"* (Romans 16:20).

Principles of offensive warfare

The dynamics of war in the spirit realm are exactly the same as war in the material realm, therefore the Bible is our battle manual and we can cease making apologies for the wars of Israel that are recorded there. In terms of spiritual warfare they take on a dramatic contemporary significance. Here are some of the important aspects that we need to take into account.

We need to prepare for battle

■ All war, including spiritual warfare is a corporate endeavor, in which the army represents the strength of the whole people, in condensed, intensified form. Therefore numbers are not important to success, but unity is (Judges 7:1–7).

■ Our personal preparedness is vital in terms of both commitment and personal holiness if we are going to overcome in a spiritual battle with the forces of evil. We need to reckon with the fact that the enemy knows us and knows our weaknesses very well.

☐ In Israel, the warrior's state was known as *kodesh*, or the "state of holiness", that is, the soldiers were separated to their task. In the life of the soldier, war takes priority over all civilian affairs (2 Timothy 2:4).

☐ For the army to have the concentrated strength that was needed for battle, every man in it had to possess absolute purity, because impurity destroys the integrity and strength of the soul. Purity is endangered by such things as:

- *Physical, sexual or religious uncleanness* (Deuteronomy 23:10–15; Numbers 5:1–4; 1 Samuel 21:5).

- *Fear.* The fearful were sent home because fear destroys morale (Deuteronomy 20:8; Judges 7:3).

- *Unfinished projects*, because they could endanger a man's separation or singleness of heart (Deuteronomy 20:5–7).

■ Spiritual warfare is a conflict of spiritual power, therefore our relationship with God is all important and it is in the place of prayer and worship that the victory is obtained.

To Israel also, spiritual power alone decided the outcome in battle. *"No king is saved by the size of his army"* (Psalm 33:16). Therefore for the army to have power, its relationship with God must be right. Thus war is ushered in by:

☐ The blowing of the silver trumpets so that *"you will be remembered by the* LORD *your God and rescued from your enemies"* (Numbers 10:9). Silver means redemption, because the basis of our victory is the Cross.

☐ The sacrifice of the burnt offering that signified worship and thanksgiving. In one sense the whole purpose of our spiritual warfare is the restoration of worship, thus reversing Satan's rebellion and reasserting God's rightful place as Creator and man's rightful place as worshiping creature. But victory for Israel also begins in the sanctuary, because it is there that strength is received.

> *"May the* LORD *answer you when you are in*
>   *distress;*
>   *may the name of the God of Jacob protect you.*
> *May he send you help from the sanctuary*
>   *and grant you support from Zion.*
> *May he remember all your sacrifices*
>   *and accept your burnt offerings.*
>
>   *Selah*

> *May he give you the desire of your heart*
> *and make all your plans succeed.*
> *We will shout for joy when you are victorious*
> *and will lift up our banners in the name*
> *of our God."* (Psalm 20:1–5)

The nature of warfare

The following principles are of critical importance for us to understand the real issues of spiritual warfare, and the means to victory.

■ To Israel, the outcome of the war depends entirely on the kings. The war is his war and, because it is spiritual power that decides the issue, victory depends on the king having victory in, his soul. His soul must be filled with victory before the battle, because the actual outcome of the battle is only the manifestation of the real victory or defeat that already exists (Psalm 18:32–34; 1 Kings 20:13ff.; 22:1ff.).

Our final victory in the spiritual warfare with Satan and his hosts is absolutely assured because Jesus Christ, our King has total victory in His soul.

> *"He must reign until he has put all his enemies under his feet."*
> (1 Corinthians 15:25; cf. Psalm 110:1–2)

Real victory already exists and the outcome of any battle is only the outward manifestation of what is already in Christ's soul.

■ The decisive spiritual thing in war is for the king to have what is called "strong counsel", that is, irresistible thoughts that are immediately carried out.

☐ By counsel is meant not just advice or suggestion, but the fullest expression of the king's mind and will, his plans, strategies, purposes, resolve and assurance.

☐ God is *"great in counsel and mighty in deed"* (Jeremiah 32:19, NASB) so His word carries in itself the power to accomplish what it declares. Therefore:

  • God's counsel, that is His plans and purposes always succeed.

    "The LORD Almighty has sworn,

    'Surely as I have planned, so it will be,
      and as I have purposed, so it will stand.' "

                                                    (Isaiah 14:24)

  • God breaks and shatters all counsel or plans directed against Him and against His people.

    "Prepare for battle, and be shattered!
      Prepare for battle, and be shattered!
    Devise your strategy, but it will be thwarted;
      propose your plan, but it will not stand,
    for God is with us."   (Isaiah 8:9–10)

  • God's counsel confuses and dissolves the enemy's counsel so that it cannot take effect. Thereby, the morale of the enemy is destroyed and his will weakened and paralyzed (Jeremiah 50:35–38; Isaiah 19:1–4).

■ The king's counsel penetrates the heart of his people and bends their will to his so that they become one soul. The victory in the king's soul becomes the victory in their soul (Revelation 12:11; John 16:33). The victory that is in Christ must penetrate our heart and soul so that His victory also becomes ours (1 John 4:4; 5:4).

"I saw Satan fall like lightning from heaven. I have given you authority to trample on snakes and scorpions and to overcome all the power of the enemy; nothing will harm you."

(Luke 10:18–19)

■ Note the importance of the prophetic ministry. In Israel, prophets played a great part in creating victory in the king's soul, because they were able to "see" whether it was there. If they could see victory or defeat it was settled as a reality! (1 Kings 22:1–40).

The critical issue in our warfare is whether we have in our soul the victory that is in Christ's soul. That is a matter of revelation. The function of the prophetic ministry is to give us the strong counsel based on revelation that will actualize that victory in us also.

The conduct of the battle

■ Remember that God directs the campaign and determines the strategy. That strategy will vary from place to place and from time to time (Joshua 5:13–15; 6:5; 8:1; Numbers 21:34; 31:1ff.; 1 Samuel 7:10; 23:2; 30:7).

■ Remember you do not have the whole front to take care of, all you have is a limited, local objective.

☐ If you do not take that objective, nobody else will do it for you.

☐ You have to do it whether you think you can or not and whether you are afraid or not.

■ Learn to use the prophetic word of Scripture as it is quickened to you by the Holy Spirit in:

☐ Speaking the judgment word of God into being against the demonic powers, or

☐ Holding the commands of God with your will against the will of the powers, or

☐ Declaring to the powers the greatness and majesty, the power and holiness, the victory and the coming again of Jesus Christ, in order to weaken and terrify them.

▪ Learn to discern the critical issues of timing in warfare.

☐ Watching for God's hand, "seeing" what the Father is doing (John 5:19).

☐ Discerning the enemy's weakness or attention lapses and capitalizing on them; seizing the momentum of a battle (2 Kings 13:14–20).

☐ Waiting for the proceeding word of God that says "Go" (1 Samuel 23:2–4).

▪ Understand the law of occupation. If you take a territory you must have the resources to hold it and to occupy it, *"or the wild animals will multiply"* (Deuteronomy 7:22).

Abijah and Jeroboam

An illustration of many of the principles of warfare that we have been discussing will be found in the account of the battle between Abijah, king of Judah and Jeroboam, king of Israel in 2 Chronicles 13:1–20.

▪ Abijah was on the defensive, because Jeroboam had superiority in numbers by 2 to 1 (verse 3) and tactical superiority; he had Abijah's army ambushed front and rear (verse 13).

■ Victory depended on the persons of the two kings. Abijah occupies the high ground (verse 4) and endeavors both to plant victory in his own soul and to plant defeat in Jeroboam's soul (verses 4–12).

■ He does this by also occupying the spiritual high ground, rehearsing the rights of Judah as the kingdom of the Lord and the Davidic dynasty (verse 8) the nation's faithfulness to the true priesthood and the true worship of God (verses 10–11). He contrasts it with Jeroboam's kingdom, born in rebellion and nurtured in idolatry.

■ When Judah found themselves under attack front and rear, they cried out to the Lord, the priests blew the silver trumpets, the warriors shouted the faith statement of the battle cry "The LORD has given our enemies into our hands" and Israel fled before Judah (verses 14–16).

■ Finally Abijah pursued Jeroboam to complete and humiliating defeat so that Jeroboam never regained his power again during Abijah's reign.

SECTION 2

Binding and Loosing

Introduction

How to make truth real

In order to convert the spiritual truth we hear or read into actual living experience, we need to find answers to the following important questions:

1. What does it actually mean?

2. How do you do it?

If our understanding as to what the truth really means is confused or defective we will always have problems in obeying it, or trying to make use of it.

If we are unclear as to what is actually involved in obeying the truth or appropriating it our best endeavors to translate belief into action are likely to miss the mark.

The lack of clear answers to the two questions is one of the main reasons for the huge gap that often exists between the truth we confess with our lips and the truth we experience as an on-going reality in our lives.

In the pages that follow we will try to address the same two important questions in relation to the subject of binding and loosing.

Understanding the Terms

Binding

The simplest and most straightforward meaning of the term *binding*, is "tying up". In this sense it is used of shackling a prisoner (Acts 12:6) or bandaging a person's wounds (Luke 10:34).

In a broader and more encompassing sense however, *binding* and related words like *bonds* and *bondage*, can be defined as:

> Restricting a person or persons in their freedom of action, choice or expression, or robbing them of their freedom, short of actual death.

Some of the words used in the New Testament to express the same, or similar meanings, are:

☐ *Restrain*: The restrainer is the Holy Spirit (2 Thessalonians 2:6–7).

☐ *Hinder*: The people responsible are the Jews (1 Thessalonians 2:16, NASB).

☐ *Thwart* or *stop*: The agent is Satan (1 Thessalonians 2:18).

☐ *Prevent*: The factor is circumstances (Romans 1:13).

☐ *Entangle*: The corruption of the world is in view (2 Peter 2:20).

☐ *Trap*: The devil is the danger (2 Timothy 2:26).

Loosing

The basic meaning of *loosing* is "untying", for example, untethering an animal (Matthew 21:2) or unwinding grave clothes (John 11:44), but it also has the more important significance of:

☐ *Release*: The object of release is the captive (Luke 4:18).

☐ *Set free*: Healing from a sickness (Luke 13:16).

☐ *Cancel* or *forgive*: The remission of debts (Luke 7:42; Matthew 6:12).

☐ *Destroy a barrier*: Discrimination between Jew and Gentile (Ephesians 2:14).

☐ *Permit*: Allow freedom of speech (Acts 21:39–40).

☐ *Liberate*: Creation freed from its bondage to corruption (Romans 8:21).

Thus we can define *loosing* as:

> Freeing a person or persons from circumstances, people or things that restrict their freedom of action, choice or expression, or rob them of their freedom.

The Bible passages

There are three main passages that are crucial for understanding what is meant by binding and loosing. The longest and most important is Matthew 16:13–20; the others are Matthew 18:15–19 and John 20:21–23.

In discussing the practical application of binding and loosing the key passages are Matthew 12:25–30 (and its parallel Mark 3:22–27) and Luke 11:14–26.

Matthew 16:13–20

> *"When Jesus came to the region of Ceasarea Philippi, he asked his disciples, 'Who do people say the Son of Man is?' They replied, 'Some say John the Baptist; others say Elijah; and still others Jeremiah or one of the prophets.'*
>
> *'But what about you?' he asked. 'Who do you say I am?'*
>
> *Simon Peter answered, 'You are the Christ, the Son of the living God.'*
>
> *Jesus replied, 'Blessed are you, Simon son of Jonah, for this was not revealed to you by man, but by my Father in heaven. And I tell you that you are Peter, and on this rock I will build my church, and the gates of Hades will not overcome it. I will give you the keys of the kingdom of heaven; whatever you bind on earth will be* [margin *"will have been"*] *bound in heaven, and whatever you loose on earth will be* [margin *"will have been"*] *loosed in heaven.'*
>
> *Then he warned his disciples not to tell anyone that he was the Christ."* (Matthew 16:13–20)

There are several very important issues dealt with in this passage that are essential for understanding the final statement of Jesus about binding and loosing.

1. The identity of Jesus

The passage begins with Jesus introducing the subject of His identity and ends with a warning to the disciples not to make that identity public for the present. The whole passage therefore hinges on who Jesus is. There were two possibilities.

The Messiah; the Christ

The Hebrew word *Messiah* corresponds to the Greek *Christos*, both signifying "anointed".

Through the collapse of Israel's national dreams and aspirations the Old Testament prophets began to discern an ultimate restoration far more glorious and extensive than the nation's wildest hopes, the coming of the Messianic age and the reign of the Lord's Anointed, the Son of David.

> *"Of the increase of his government and peace*
> *there will be no end.*
> *He will reign on David's throne*
> *and over his kingdom,*
> *establishing and upholding it*
> *with justice and righteousness*
> *from that time on and for ever."*   (Isaiah 9:7)

The prophets stretched the capacity of language to express their vision of that coming age. The wolf would live with the lamb, the infant would play near the cobra's hole. Men would beat their swords into plowshares, their spears into pruning hooks, and the nations would train for war no more.

> *"They will neither harm nor destroy*
> *on all my holy mountain,*
> *for the earth will be full of the knowledge of the* LORD
> *as the waters cover the sea."*   (Isaiah 11:9)

The prophet like Moses; the Suffering Servant

The prophets saw clearly, however, that if the Kingdom came in its holiness, it would confirm everything in harmony with it but it would destroy everything not in harmony with its holiness. They spoke of men crawling into holes in the ground and calling on the rocks to cover them from the "great and terrible day of the Lord". They were also speaking about the coming of the Messianic age.

But in struggling with the tension of the coming Kingdom and the fate of sinners, they saw the emergence of another figure, the prophet like Moses (Deuteronomy 18:18), the Suffering Servant, who would take up our infirmities and carry our sorrows, whose life would be made a guilt offering and who would justify many because He would bear their iniquity (Isaiah 53:1–12).

The Jews of Jesus' day thought that these were two different persons. When John the Baptist confessed freely, *"I am not the Christ,"* the question was, *"Are you the Prophet?"* (John 1:20–21). With Jesus Himself there was an on-going controversy as to whether He was the Christ or the Prophet (John 4:29; 6:14).

John the Baptist's first revelation concerning Jesus was that He was the Suffering Servant, the Lamb of God, who takes away the sin of the world (John 1:29). Only later in prison, when he heard of the miraculous works of Jesus, did he begin to think that He could also be the Messiah (Matthew 11:1–7).

Peter's revelation, on the other hand, was that Jesus of Nazareth was the Messiah, the Christ, the Lord's Anointed King (Matthew 16:16). Later, when Jesus began to explain that He was also the Suffering Servant, Peter had serious problems with accepting that revelation (Matthew 16:22).

■ *Point 1: Jesus of Nazareth is the Christ, the Messiah, the Lord's Anointed King of the Kingdom of God.*

2. The Rock

Because Peter is moving in revelation knowledge, Jesus takes him a step further into truth. The controversy that has surrounded the question of Peter and the rock disappears if we balance the statements made by Jesus and Peter about each other.

You are:	*You are:*
Peter	the Christ
the son of Jonah	the Son of the living God
Peter (*petros*, a stone)	the Rock (*petra*, mass of rock)

Moreover, the meaning would be abundantly clear to the disciples because "the Rock" was one of the very well known names of God in the Old Testament (Deuteronomy 32:13, 15, 18, 30; 1 Samuel 2:2; 2 Samuel 22:2; 23:3; Psalm 18:31; Isaiah 26:4; 30:29; Habakkuk 1:12).

> *"I will proclaim the name of the* LORD.
>   *Oh, praise the greatness of our God!*
> *He is the Rock, his works are perfect,*
>   *and all his ways are just."*

(Deuteronomy 32:3–4)

Furthermore, Paul, looking back to the wilderness experiences when Moses brought water out of the rock (Exodus 17:6; Numbers 20:8), declares unequivocally *"that rock was Christ"* (1 Corinthians 10:4).

■ *Point 2: Jesus of Nazareth is not only the Messiah King, He is the Rock of Israel, that is, God in Person and the foundation and builder of the church.*

3. The gates of Hades

Hades is the place of departed spirits and is here spoken of as the city of death. Death and Hades always go together, even to the final judgment in the lake of fire (Revelation 1:18; 6:8; 20:13–14).

In ancient times the gates of the city were not only the means of entry and access but also the strategic key for conquering or controlling the city. Thus a person who is dying is said to *"[draw] near the gates of death"* (Psalm 107:18) and capturing the city is "possessing the gates of your enemies" (Genesis 22:17, ASB).

Because of their strength and importance, the gates represent the power of the city. Thus the gates of Hades are *"the powers of death"* (RSV), *"the powers of the unseen"* (Con. Lit.), *"the forces of death"* (Moffatt) or the kingdom of death.

■ **Point 3:** *Jesus Christ, the Rock of Israel, the Messianic King of the Kingdom of God is the foundation of the Church, and is victorious over the strongest powers of the unseen realm, the kingdom of death itself.*

4. The keys of the Kingdom
Note that the Kingdom of Heaven and the Kingdom of God are expressions meaning the same thing, the reign or rule of God. (Compare Matthew 13:31–32 with Mark 4:30–32 and Matthew 4:17 with Mark 1:15.) Matthew uses the rabbinical term in which heaven is a roundabout way of saying God.

In Scripture, the key is the symbol of authority. Thus Jesus is spoken of as having,

☐ *"The keys of death and Hades"* (Revelation 1:18), that is, **authority over death and hell**.

☐ *"The key of David"* (Revelation 3:7; see Isaiah 22:20–23), that is, **the key or authority of the Kingdom**. He opens and no one shuts, He shuts and no one opens.

The keys of the Kingdom are the authority to exercise the power of the Kingdom to bring to pass on earth the kind of effects that take place in heaven. It means putting into effect what is expressed in the Lord's prayer:

> *"your kingdom come,*
> *your will be done*
> *on earth as it is in heaven."*   (Matthew 6:10)

The keys lock heaven and earth together in power to accomplish that result.

■ *Point 4: Jesus, the Messianic King, the Rock of Israel, gives to His disciples the authority of the Kingdom, to bring the reign and rule of God to pass, on earth as it is in heaven.*

5. Binding and loosing

The means whereby this accomplishing of God's rule on earth is to be achieved is by **binding and loosing**. That is, **by restricting on earth those things that are restricted or restrained in heaven and by liberating or setting free on earth those things that are set free in heaven**. Thus earth follows heaven, and heaven dictates the course of action on earth. What this involves will come clearer as we go on.

Matthew 18:15–19

The larger context of this passage occupies the whole of chapter 18 and its setting in that chapter is the key to understanding verses 15 to 19.

The chief topic is again the Kingdom of God. It begins with the question of the disciples as to who is the greatest in the Kingdom. Jesus answers by calling a child to Him and speaking about:

☐ Becoming a child to enter the Kingdom (verse 3).

☐ Humbling oneself like a child to be the greatest in the Kingdom (verse 4).

☐ Welcoming a child is welcoming the King of the Kingdom (verse 5).

Then the child (Greek *paidon*) becomes a symbol for all the little ones (Greek *micros*), that is, all those who are small or little in age, situation, rank or reputation – the humble folk and the new believers. Jesus speaks about:

☐ Causing a little one to stumble (verse 6).

☐ Looking down on the little ones (verse 7).

☐ Seeking for the little one gone astray, the lost sheep (verses 10–14).

Immediately after the parable of the lost sheep, Jesus goes on to say:

> *"If your brother sins against you, go and show him his fault, just between the two of you. If he listens to you, you have won your brother over. But if he will not listen, take one or two others along, so that 'every matter may be established by the testimony of two or three witnesses.' If he refuses to listen to them, tell it to the church; and if he refuses to listen even to the church, treat him as you would a pagan or a tax collector.*
>
> *I tell you the truth, whatever you bind on earth will be* [margin *"will have been"*] *bound in heaven, and whatever you loose on earth will be* [margin *"will have been"*] *loosed in heaven.*
>
> *Again, I tell you that if two of you on earth agree about anything you ask for, it will be done for you by my Father in heaven. For where two or three come together in my name, there am I with them."*   (Matthew 18:15–20)

Here are the important points in understanding this passage:

■ **The primary aim is the winning over and recovery of the sinning brother** who is a sheep that has gone astray.

If unity and concord are restored, earth comes into harmony with heaven and whatever is asked for will be granted. It will be granted because the request will be precisely for those kind of things that are approved in heaven.

■ *If the individual approach to reconciliation fails, the sinning brother is not to be abandoned* but sought by means of corporate counsel from two or three together, or failing that by the Church as a whole.

This is because when two or three gather in the Name of Christ, they represent His authority and secure the presence amongst them of the Lord of heaven, the King of the Kingdom.

■ *If the final approach fails, the sinning brother is to be treated as a pagan or a tax collector.* Note that this does not mean that he is to be shunned or ostracized, because Jesus was a friend of tax gatherers and sinners and Matthew himself was once one of them.

Nor does it mean withholding forgiveness because Jesus goes on to tell the parable of the unmerciful servant to show the long-suffering nature of true forgiveness.

It means however that the offender has separated himself from the community of faith and while he remains the object of evangelism and intercession, he is no longer the object of fellowship within the body.

■ *In this context binding and loosing becomes a matter of church discipline*, but discipline must be exercised not out of personal hurt or grievance but in the authority of the King-dom of God and therefore on the basis of what the Kingdom allows and what the Kingdom forbids.

Moreover the first application of binding and loosing should be redemptive, that is restricting or restraining the influences that make for strife and division and releasing the affected parties from those influences or circumstances so that reconciliation may be achieved.

John 20:19–23

The words "bind" and "loose" are not used as such in this passage, but forgive and retain are common synonyms for loose and bind when used of either money debts or moral debts or obligations (Matthew 6:12; 18:27; Romans 1:14).

> *"On the evening of that first day of the week, when the disciples were together, with the doors locked for fear of the Jews, Jesus came and stood among them and said, 'Peace be with you.' After he said this, he showed them his hands and side. The disciples were overjoyed when they saw the Lord.*
>
> *Again Jesus said, 'Peace be with you! As the Father has sent me, I am sending you.' And with that he breathed on them and said, 'Receive the Holy Spirit. If you forgive anyone his sins, they are forgiven; if you do not forgive them, they are not forgiven."* (John 20:19–23)

There is the same sequence of authorization and empowering here as in the previous passages, but here heaven and earth are held together by the presence of the One who holds the keys of the Kingdom. The two or three are gathered and Jesus is in their midst.

1. Authorization
"As the Father has sent me, I am sending you" (verse 21). Just as the Father gave authority to the Son (John 5:27) so now the Son gives His authority to the disciples.

2. Empowering
"Receive the Holy Spirit" (verse 22). In the life and ministry of Jesus the Holy Spirit was the *"power of the Lord"* (Luke 5:17). Access to the same power is now given to the disciples by the presence of the same Holy Spirit.

3. Application

The NASB translation of verse 23 (margin) echoes that of Matthew 16 and Matthew 18:

> *"If you forgive the sins of any, their sins have previously been forgiven them; if you retain the sins of any, they have previously been retained."*

When the keys of the Kingdom lock together earth and heaven (the unseen spiritual dimension of reality where Christ reigns and the Kingdom functions in fullness) (Ephesians 1:19–23):

☐ The decisions of earth follow the decisions of heaven.

☐ The activities of earth follow the activities of heaven.

☐ The judgments of earth follow the judgments of heaven.

☐ The declarations of earth follow the declarations of heaven.

In all these situations the will and purposes of God are paramount and the Holy Spirit is the revealer of that will and those purposes.

Summary of the biblical passages

The Church has been given authority (the keys of the Kingdom) and is empowered by the Holy Spirit to bring into being on earth the conditions that apply in heaven, that is accomplishing the will of God on earth as it is in heaven. The scope of this authority extends to:

☐ Binding and loosing demons, sickness and circumstances (Matthew 16:13–20).

☐ Binding and loosing behavior, church discipline (Matthew 18:15–19).

☐ Forgiving and retaining sins (John 20:19–23).

The Scope of Binding and Loosing

In chapter 9 we defined binding and loosing as restricting freedom of action on the one hand, and releasing from such restrictions on the other.

Firstly note that binding, or bringing into bondage, is bad when a person is bound by demons or sickness or debt. But it is good when a person feels bound to keep a promise or when it means restricting the freedom of evil spirits or evil men.

Loosing is good when it means releasing someone from their fears or addictions or from demonization, but it is bad when it means letting our mouth loose in evil (Psalm 50:19) or our behavior in loose living.

Secondly, remember that Satan also is engaged in binding and loosing wherever he can (1 Thessalonians 2:18, ASB). The outcome therefore depends on who is doing the binding and loosing and what is being bound and loosed. As far as we are concerned we are to

☐ Bind what God binds and loose what Satan binds

☐ Loose what God looses and bind what Satan looses

Thirdly, the two activities often go together. To loose a person from the power of an evil spirit will usually involve binding or restricting the freedom or action of the evil spirit (Mark 1:32–34; 9:25).

Binding or bondages

The detailed analysis of bondages in the New Testament is an indication of the importance of the subject. It also reveals that most of the binding being done is being done by Satan and that the main exercise of our authority is to loose people from their bondages.

■ *The bonds may be literal*

☐ Material shackles or fetters (Luke 8:29).

☐ The condition of imprisonment, captivity or servitude (Matthew 18:25; 2 Corinthians 6:5; Philippians 1:7, 13; Titus 2:9).

■ *They may be bodily conditions that restrict a person's freedom of action or expression*

☐ Impediments such as blindness, deafness or speech difficulties (Matthew 15:14; Mark 7:32).

☐ Paralysis or other crippling infirmities (Luke 13:16).

■ *The restraints may be imposed by law*

☐ The purpose of law is to restrain evil in society, and in other areas it sets bounds or limits on individual freedom. For example in marriage law and partnership law (Romans 7:2; 2 Corinthians 6:14).

☐ The law may, however, be used to restrict the Gospel (Acts 9:1–3).

■ *The bond may be a moral one*, that is, the person is restricted in what they feel free to do, not by any outside force but by an inner restraint. This is important when we come to discuss the nature of the authority we exercise which is mainly a moral and spiritual authority.

☐ A person may bind themselves by a promise or an oath or vow (Acts 20:22ff.).

☐ Or they may have such a strong inner conviction as to what they should do, that they feel they must do it no matter what the cost (Acts 23:12, 21).

☐ Conscience functions as an internalized law to restrain our behavior even in the absence of external law (Romans 2:14).

☐ A person may feel "duty bound", that is bound by a sense of duty or obligation to do something or go somewhere (Romans 1:14).

■ *The bondage may be psychological*

☐ Addiction to alcohol, drugs, gambling, etc. (1 Timothy 3:8).

☐ Slavery to certain moods or emotions such as fear, anxiety, anger, rejection or depression (Proverbs 19:19; Isaiah 54:6; Hebrews 2:14–15).

☐ Domination or manipulation by other people through force of will, personality, emotion or peer pressure.

■ *The bondage may be spiritual*, for example:

☐ Sinful habits or sensuality (Titus 3:3; 2 Peter 2:19).

☐ Passivity of mind or will (2 Timothy 2:26). The person is enslaved or captive and seemingly cannot take any steps towards freedom or see through the deception.

☐ Occult bondage (Acts 8:23–24) through involvement in spiritism, witchcraft, magic, pagan religions or societies that are wholly or partly under occult control or involved in occult practices.

☐ Demonization, where the person is under demonic control, either wholly or partly and either temporarily or permanently (Mark 5:1–13).

☐ Curses, that is, words of malediction or evil speaking that have become the vehicles for evil spirits to intervene (Luke 6:28; 1 Samuel 17:43).

☐ Inner vows that become self-imposed curses or self-fulfilling prophecies because they echo our own inner fears or doubts (Proverbs 26:2).

■ *Circumstances may bind a person so that they have little freedom of action*

☐ Indebtedness or poverty, including the "poverty trap", that is, the very poor who need education and skills to get out of their predicament, but lack the money to get training, are unable to move in search of jobs, and have health and nutrition levels that incapacitate them for hard work.

☐ Other sets of circumstances sometimes force our hand and leave us few if any options from which to choose.

Who or what are we to bind?

We are to bind on earth whatever the Kingdom of God binds in the heavenlies.

■ *Satan and the demonic hierarchy of powers* (Ephesians 6:12) Behind the structures of society is the demonic overlay of rulers, authorities, powers and spiritual forces of evil in the unseen, spiritual realm. These are enslaving the human race and interfering with the response of people, institutions and societies to the Gospel (Mark 9:25; Revelation 20:1–2).

☐ Geographical, over nations, states, cities, territories and land areas (1 Kings 11:5; 2 Kings 17:29–31; Isaiah 21:9; Daniel 10:13, 20).

☐ Over spheres of influence, for example Mammon in relation to money, Moloch in relation to abortion, Aphrodite in relation to sex, etc.

■ *Demons or evil spirits* involved in the demonization of individuals and groups such as spiritists, covens, adherents of pagan religions and occult societies.

■ *Principalities and powers.* That is the structural manifestations of power in society, governments, bureaucracies, business corporations, national cultures, media, educational institutions, etc. (see Section 1).

There is an inner, corporate spirit or persona in these powers that is fallen but not demonic and that is in rebellion against the Lordship of Christ. This rebellion and the actions and influence of the powers are to be restrained where they are in opposition to the Kingdom of God.

■ *The actions, influences and attitudes of people* where they are the instruments of evil or oppression in society. For example pornography, prostitution, abortion, drug traffic, greed and corruption. The powers, in "Principalities and powers" above, are created by people and live and work in and through people.

■ *Circumstances, sickness, conditions and influences* that are in opposition to the will of God, stand in the way of His purposes, hinder the spread of the Gospel or bring suffering and affliction into people's lives.

Who or what are we to loose?

■ *People*, setting them free from their bondages, sicknesses, inhibitions, fears and sins and releasing them to fulfill their God-given potential in serving Him. People may need to be set free in their:

☐ Human spirit so as to be able to hear from God, worship God and operate effectively in the realm of spiritual gifts and graces.

☐ Mind, so that it is freed from compulsive thoughts and renewed by the Holy Spirit.

☐ Will, from addictions and enslaving habits.

☐ Emotions, from inner hurts, fears and inhibitions.

☐ Bodies from physical, psychosomatic and spiritually-based sicknesses and disabilities.

☐ Relationships, in marriages, families, churches, and social groupings.

■ *Principalities and powers*. The creational or structural powers, that is the organizations and institutions of human societies, which are fallen but not demonic, need to be loosed from the demonic powers so that they are opened up to change and can be called back to fulfill their God-ordained functions and destinies in the Kingdom of God. We need therefore to:

☐ Cast demons out of the structures and out of the geographical or geopolitical spheres in the world.

☐ Address the structures of nations and societies with the claims of the Lordship of Jesus Christ.

■ **Resources** of money, facilities, land, equipment, personnel, materials and ideas that are required for the work of the Kingdom of God.

First Bind the Strong Man

In Matthew 12 Jesus is involved in a controversy with the Pharisees who claimed He was casting out demons by Beelzebul or Satan, the prince of the demons. In the course of His reply Jesus made this statement:

> *"Any kingdom divided against itself is laid waste; and any city or house divided against itself will not stand. If Satan casts out Satan, he is divided against himself; how then will his kingdom stand? If I by Beelzebul cast out demons, by whom do your sons cast them out? For this reason they will be your judges. But if I cast out demons by the Spirit of God, then the kingdom of God has come upon you.*
>
> *Or how can anyone enter the strong man's house and carry off his property, unless he first binds the strong man? And then he will plunder his house."*
>
> (Matthew 12:25–29, NASB)

In dealing with the matter of binding and loosing, Jesus establishes a very important principle:

☐ **First things first – first bind the strong man**

Many of our common approaches to counseling or problems come at the situation from exactly the opposite approach first the flesh, then emotional problems, then relational difficulties, then generational ties, and lastly if there is an unexplainable remainder, consider the possibility of demonization in one form or another.

Jesus says this is like trying to rob a strong man's house while the strong man is still there, and unhampered in his activity.

If demonic strongholds are not dealt with first, the common experience will be that:

☐ They will bring confusion and chaos into the process of trying to diagnose what the real problems are. The more you probe, the more entangled and perplexing the matter becomes.

☐ They will strongly resist and hinder the attempts of the person to deal with the problems or to open themselves to the grace of God.

Who is the strong man?

The New Testament discloses, not a mere principle of evil in the universe, but a highly organized and powerful kingdom, implacably opposed to the will of God and determined to hold man and the world in slavery.

This kingdom of darkness consists of:

1. Satan, the prince or ruler
Satan, the fallen archangel (Ezekiel 28:11–17) is described as the prince or ruler of the demons (Matthew 9:34, 12:24). When Adam fell, he lost his authority over the world, and into the spiritual vacuum that was left Satan came, becoming the god and ruler of this world (John 12:31; 14:30; 16:11; 2 Corinthians 4:4).

His names reveal his character. Satan, the adversary (1 Peter 5:8), devil, the accuser or slanderer (Revelation 12:10), the evil one (1 John 5:19), the enemy (Luke 10:19), also the deceiver (Revelation 20:10), murderer and the father of lies (John 8:44). He is likened to a serpent (2 Corinthians 11:3), a dragon (Revelation 13:2), and a roaring lion (1 Peter 5:8)!

In his kingdom of darkness, Satan has a throne (Revelation 2:13; 13:2), and fortresses (2 Corinthians 10:4); he has the power to perform signs and wonders (2 Thessalonians 2:9), the power or strength of death (Hebrews 2:14), and deep mysteries of evil (2 Thessalonians 2:7; Revelation 2:24).

Satan is however neither omnipotent nor omnipresent. He cannot be in more than one place at the same time. He operates through a vast host of fallen angels (2 Peter 2:4; Jude 1:6), spirit beings also called demons (Luke 8:27), evil spirits (Luke 11:24–26), and unclean spirits (Mark 9:25).

They are organized as described below.

2. A hierarchy or structure of evil powers

This structure is nowhere exhaustively described in Scripture but is referred to in a range of categories and terms. One way of interpreting the rich variety of information is as follows:

■ *Powers that are geopolitical or geographical*

☐ World rulers (*kosmokrator*; Ephesians 6:12) – probably the highest order of powers.

☐ Principalities (*arche*) or rulerships – perhaps the gods of the nations or other territories (Deuteronomy 32:8–9, RSV; Daniel 10:13, 20; perhaps Acts 16:9).

☐ Rulers (*archon*; 1 Corinthians 2:6, 8; Colossians 1:16) – lower orders of geographical or territorial powers, perhaps over specific institutions, etc.

■ *Powers that are over areas or spheres of influence*

☐ Dominions or lordships (*kuriotes*) – for example, the media, money and wealth (mammon) cultures, academic disciplines, legal systems, etc.

☐ Powers (*dunamis*; Romans 8:38) – including the spiritual force (*pneumatikos*) of evil in the spiritual realm.

☐ Authorities (*exousia*; Colossians 2:15; 1 Peter 3:22) – beings with the right to use power delegated from the higher orders above them.

The picture is that of a close-knit network of power structures, heavily dependent on one another and on the power of Satan and the world rulers. While Satan is *the* strong man, there will also be in any specific territory, or set of circumstances, or demonized individual, a "strong man" who represents the power source and the dominating influence in that particular situation. He will be the key to setting the situation free.

Jesus and the strong man

When Jesus says, "First bind the strong man", He is speaking out of a hard-won experience. The very first thing that Jesus did after He was baptized and filled with the Holy Spirit was to seek out the strong man, Satan himself, in the wilderness (Matthew 4:1–11).

■ There, in the most unfavorable conditions, the wilderness, not a garden like Eden, not freshly rested but after fasting forty days and nights, He met all the subtlety and deceptive seduction of the fallen archangel, not in one temptation but in three, and came off victorious.

■ Jesus faced Satan, eyeball to eyeball, as a Spirit-filled Man and **established, once and for all, His moral ascendancy over the** *evil one*. The devil met his match. At the beginning it was the tempter who came to Jesus, at the end it was Jesus who had mastered the tempter and dismissed him peremptorily from His presence. "Get out of here Satan!"

■ **Satan was bound**, that is, his heretofore absolute freedom over the world was now limited, because he knew that if it came to a show-down this Man's will would overmaster his every time. Such confrontations he could no longer afford. Henceforth he would have to work indirectly against Jesus, through Peter, through Judas, through the powers, through the elements, to destroy the Man who would thwart him at every turn. That plan was, as we will see, his final undoing.

And plunder his house

After His binding of the strong man in the wilderness, Jesus returned to Galilee in the power of the Spirit (Luke 4:14), came to Nazareth, and in the synagogue declared His manifesto.

> "The Spirit of the Lord is on me,
>   because he has anointed me
>   to preach good news to the poor.
> He has sent me to proclaim freedom for the prisoners
>   and recovery of sight for the blind,
> to release the oppressed,
>   to proclaim the year of the Lord's favour."
>
> (Luke 4:18–19)

His public ministry fulfilled this declaration.

■ **He went around the synagogues, casting out demons**. He forbade the demon to speak, *"Be quiet! ... Come out of him!"* (Luke 4:35); commanded a deaf and dumb spirit, *"Come out of* him and never enter him again" (Mark 9:25); and at other times forbidding the demons to speak, because they knew who He was (Mark 1:34). The demons recognized His authority and obeyed Him, even seeking His permission before they dared to go into the swine at Gadara (Luke 8:32).

■ **Where evil spirits had afflicted the bodies of men and women he released them.**

> "Should not this woman, a daughter of Abraham, whom Satan has bound for eighteen long years, be set free on the Sabbath day from what bound her?"   (Luke 13:16)

■ **In the storm on the lake, Jesus discerned the demonic source of the tempest.** He rebuked the wind and literally "muzzled" the sea (Mark 4:39) in exactly the same manner as He dealt with the unclean demon in the synagogue (Luke 4:34).

> "All the people were amazed and said to each other, 'What is this teaching? With authority and power he gives orders to evil spirits and they come out!' "   (Luke 4:36)

■ **Having established His unchallenged ascendancy over Satan and the demons, He authorizes His disciples to act in His name and likewise to cast out demons** (Luke 9:1–2).

When the seventy disciples come back with joy saying "Even the demons submit to us in your name" (Luke 10:17), He explained the reason for this,

> "I saw Satan fall like lightning from heaven." (Luke 10:18)

What His disciples had been doing was plundering the strong man's house after the strong man had been bound and inhibited.

■ *The ascendancy and authority that Jesus established over Satan and the demons was declared by Him to be through the presence in Him of the Holy Spirit and to be evidence of the coming of the Kingdom of God.*

> *"But if I drive out demons by the Spirit of God, then the kingdom of God has come upon you."*   (Matthew 12:28)

In other words, Jesus was doing on earth the things that were already being done in heaven.

> *"I tell you the truth, the Son can do nothing by himself; he can do only what he sees his Father doing."*   (John 5:19)

The victory of the Cross

In 1 Corinthians 2 Paul is speaking of the hidden wisdom in the Cross of Christ,

> *"None of the rulers of this age understood it, for if they had they would not have crucified the Lord of glory."*
> (1 Corinthians 2:8)

The rulers of this age, who are coming to nothing (1 Corinthians 2:6) are the satanic powers who engineered the death of Jesus. What Paul is saying is that if Satan had had any idea of what was going to happen on the Cross, he would have leveled every tree in Palestine rather than let them use one to crucify the Lord of glory. Satan never understood until too late that the Cross was the ultimate and irreversible binding of his power and restriction of his freedom to act.

■ *By His death and His resurrection from the dead, Jesus robbed Satan of his ultimate weapon against the human race.*

"Since then the children share in flesh and blood, He himself likewise also partook of the same, that through death he might render powerless [Greek katargeo] him who had the power of death, that is, the devil, and might free those who through fear of death were subject to slavery all their lives."

(Hebrews 2:14–15, NASB)

■ **By His ultimate obedience to death, even death on the Cross (Philippians 2:8) Jesus met and exhausted the rebellion of the principalities and powers,**

"When He had disarmed [Greek katargeo] the rulers and authorities, He made a public display of them having triumphed over them through Him."   (Colossians 2:15, NASB)

Now Jesus has obtained ultimate authority in heaven and on earth after angels and rulers and authorities and powers have been brought into submission under him (1 Peter 3:22, NASB)

■ **By the redeeming power of his blood Jesus has delivered us from the authority of darkness** and God has *"transferred us to the kingdom of His beloved Son"* (Colossians, 1:13 NASB). We have been changed from rebellious and disobedient enemies to loving sons and daughters thus robbing Satan, the ruler of the kingdom of the air, the spirit who is now at work in those who are disobedient (Ephesians 2:2) of his ground in our lives.

■ **The work of Jesus in dispossessing Satan of his hold on mankind is to be carried on in this age by his followers, exercising His authority in His name by the power of His Spirit.**
The reason the Son of God appeared was to destroy (literally, "loose") the devil's work (1 John 3:8).

"Truly, truly, I say to you, he who believes in Me, the works that I do, he will do also; and greater works than these he will do; because I go to the Father." (John 14:12, NASB)

"Behold I have given you authority to tread on serpents and scorpions, and over all the power of the enemy, and nothing will injure you." (Luke 10:19, NASB)

How to Bind the Strong Man

When it comes to binding the strong man, Jesus does not leave us with only vague ideas about what is meant. In Luke 11 He goes into very precise detail as to what it means and how it is to be done.

> *"When a strong man, fully armed, guards his own house, his possessions are safe. But when someone stronger attacks and overpowers him, he takes away the armour in which the man trusted and divides up the spoils."* (Luke 11:21)

Here are the important steps that are involved.

1. Identify the strong man

In every place or set of circumstances, or even in an individual life, there will be a demonic power that controls the situation, organizes the defense and is the primary source of power or energy for other spirits that may be involved. Some indicators as to the identity of the strong man are:

The armor (panopleia) he is wearing

The word *panopleia* is used only twice in the New Testament.

In Ephesians 6:11–18 it refers to the full armor of God and in Luke 11:22 it refers to the full armor of Satan.

☐ The full armor of God is a set of life conditions that God wants to establish in our life which will enable God to work in us and will prevent or restrict Satan working in us.

☐ The full armor of Satan is a set of life conditions that Satan wants to establish in our life which will allow him to work in us and will prevent or restrict God from working in us.

The life conditions of Satan will be the reverse of the life conditions God wants to establish.

The full armor of God	*The full armor of Satan*
Truth	Lies, deception
Peace	Strife, contention
Righteousness (right relatedness)	Alienation, rejection
Faith	Mistrust, suspicion, doubt
Hope	Despair, depression
The Word of God	Human reasoning
Prayer	Occultic meditation

If we can identify the major components of the life conditions in the individual or the institution we may be able to work back from them to identify the character of the strong man.

The state of the "house"
When demons enter and dwell in a person, it is called their "house" (Luke 11:24–26). The same is true of an institution or a geopolitical entity such as a city. What is implied is that there is some correspondence between the state or condition of the "house" and the nature of its occupants. Thus

Scripture identifies a deaf and dumb spirit (Mark 9:25), an unclean spirit (Luke 4:33), a spirit of divination (Acts 16:16), and so on.

The name

In Scripture a name always indicates an identity or a character. For this reason the name of the strong man is sometimes the key to taking effective action against him and on occasions you find Jesus demanding the name of the demon in control of other demons. This is clearly the case with the Gadarene demoniac. Jesus treats the spirit as an individual, *"Come out of the man, you unclean spirit!"* (Mark 5:8, RSV) and it speaks in the singular, *"What have you to do with me? . . . do not torment me . . . My name is Legion"* (Mark 5:7, 9, RSV). Then it is the demons (plural) who beg Jesus not to send them out of the area. Jesus gave them permission to enter the swine, and the evil spirits came out of the man and into the animals (Mark 5:12–13). Legion was the name of the strong man who controlled and empowered the host of other demons in the man.

Note, however, that Jesus did not always ask for the name, although it is clear He always knew the nature of the spirits He was dealing with.

The nature of the demonic strong man may also be revealed through the spiritual gifts of a word of knowledge or the discernment of spirits.

2. Get more power on your side than the strong man has

In Ephesians 6:10–18 Paul emphasizes what Jesus also asserts, that engaging and overcoming the strong man is by no means a pushover. It is neither metaphorical war or make believe war, it is real war, therefore the passage is full of strong imperatives like "struggle", "withstand", "be strong", "keep alert", "the evil day", and so on.

Our strength lies in our confidence in the absolute victory of the death and resurrection of Christ over Satan and all his hosts, and our personal relationship with the Victor Himself. It also rests in the certainty of the authority that has been given to us to preach the Gospel, heal the sick and cast out demons.

But we still need the full armor of God – that is the life conditions that enable us to overcome. But life conditions require appropriation and obedience to take effect, therefore our capacity for the task of binding a particular strong man always has a relativity about it. We may find that we are tackling more than we can manage on our own, therefore we must never hesitate to call in help. In fact, warfare is always a corporate activity and victory goes to the side that can muster superior strength (Romans 13:12–14; Ephesians 6:10).

3. Get on the attack

One of the common manifestations of demonic control is the passivity that is induced; the person's will is inert, the mind is dull and the spirit is torpid and lifeless. From the strong man's perspective, everything is undisturbed and at peace. The perils of passivity from our point of view, however, is that it gives all the initiative over to Satan and loses the battle by default.

Even defense is inadequate – that is, fight only when you are attacked. Defense at best only prevents defeat, it will never win a war. The biblical principle is always attack, which is why the Bible gives no instructions for fortifying a defensive position. Joshua goes out to fight Amalek, David runs out to meet Goliath, and Jesus goes out into the wilderness to encounter Satan.

Attack seizes the initiative from the enemy, dictates the terms of battle and chooses the ground on which it will be fought. The grounds of our victory are the grounds of Calvary.

"For the accuser of our brothers,
　　who accuses them before our God day and night,
　　has been hurled down.
They overcame him
　　by the blood of the Lamb
　　and by the word of their testimony."

(Revelation 12:10–11)

The strong man's position is vulnerable, but it is vulnerable only to attack.

4. Overpower him

The attack must be pressed until the strong man is overpowered. Even in the ministry of Jesus it seems that deliverance was not always an instantaneous thing, there was resistance and arguing and sometimes the action of Jesus is in the continuous, *"He* [had been saying] *to him, 'Come out of the man, you unclean spirit!' "* (Mark 5:8, RSV).

We will discuss more fully later the nature of the power that is involved in binding and loosing, but here we need to emphasize that ultimate victory comes by insisting that God's will be done on earth as it is in heaven. We need to persist in that stance until resistance crumbles, as ultimately it must.

5. Take away the armor in which the man trusted

That means dealing with the life conditions that have enabled the strong man to maintain his position. When the strong man is bound, and often only after the strong man is bound, we can get access to the specific life problems that need to be dealt with. This is critical in order to dismantle the demonic strongholds (2 Corinthians 10:4) and to set the person free. It will involve:

■ *Freeing the person's will* so that it can make wholehearted choices for Christ against Satan and satanic bondages. No matter how buried the person's will is, there remains the freedom of moral choice that God always protects.

■ **Dealing one by one with sins, enslaving habits, occult bondages, fears and other problems.** Often there will be a tangle that has to be carefully unpicked.

■ **Repentance, forgiveness, cleansing and the re-ordering of the person's thought patterns and lifestyle**, replacing the demonic life conditions with the armor of God, the life conditions that God wants to establish.

As the strongholds are broken down and the life conditions are changed there may well be successive deliverances from evil spirits associated with these states. Cut off from the power of the strong man however, they can generally be dealt with very easily, or they may leave of their own accord.

6. Divide up the spoils

The purpose of binding is to loose. Getting rid of demonic control and infestation is the negative aspect, releasing the life into the fullness of its potential is the positive side, that is loosing.

A person's problems are almost always a pointer to their best potential because Satan will try to spoil a life along the line of its greatest strengths. We need to release life and creativity into those atrophied areas that have been denied expression so that the person can begin to become all that God created them to be. That is enjoying the spoils of war in a spiritual sense.

The Word of God and the Authority of the Believer

Before we can effectively bind anybody or anything, or for that matter loose or release anyone who is bound, we have to know how the process works and what we are actually dealing with. Otherwise we will fall into the trap of thinking that all we have done is to recite the correct formula and things will happen. We soon discover that nothing happens, no matter how loud we shout or what words we use.

For our present purpose we can ignore physical chains or imprisonment because you cannot chain a demon or put an evil spirit in a prison cell. We therefore have to consider the ways in which a person's freedom can be taken away or restricted without the use of actual physical force. There are three means that are relevant:

1. Law

2. Authority

3. Spiritual power

The force of law

Law has the power to restrict our freedom of action in anything it orders us to do or in anything it prohibits us from doing. Law does not ask for our agreement with its demands, nor does it consult our preferences, or priorities. It claims that we "ought" to do what it says, whether we like it or not, and it is prepared, if necessary, to penalize or punish infractions in order to enforce its commands.

We may readily obey the requirements of the law because we agree with them as being good law and consider that everybody else should also obey. In that case there is no sense of restriction on our freedom, because we freely choose to do the things that the law requires. We are not conscious of the law having any binding effect on us because we obey it willingly. That is the way in which we, as Christians, have been enabled to live in the freedom of obedience to the law of God.

In other cases, however, we obey the law, in the sense of complying with its demands, but we do so only because we do not want to be penalized or punished for breaking the law. Our freedom, in other words, is limited or restricted by the coercive power wielded by the law.

When we make a promise or a vow to do something, or not to do something, our freedom of choice or action is also restricted by that promise because we feel "bound" in conscience to keep our word. The force of conscience is like that of an internalized law, but it has positive responses as well as negative ones. In this it differs from external law which does not reward us for keeping its commands but only penalizes us if we do not. On the other hand, conscience commends us when we do what it approves (Acts 24:16; 1 Peter 3:16) – we have a "good conscience" about it. But like the law, conscience penalizes us if we disobey it, it accuses us (Romans 2:15), and lets us experience unpleasant feelings of guilt and failure.

Satan and the Word of God

Satan is bound, that is, his freedom of action, and the freedom of the demons is restricted when they are confronted with the

Word of God. Sometimes it is said that Satan is a legalist, but it is not that he respects the law, he fears the Lawgiver. That was the dreadful, crippling effect on him of the words of Jesus, *"It is written . . . "* (Luke 4:4). James describes the reaction of the demons likewise:

> *"You believe that there is one God. Good! Even the demons believe that – and shudder."*   (James 2:19)

One of the primary means of binding Satan and the demons is by the use of the Word of God, the sword of the Spirit (Ephesians 6:17).

■ **The Word of God is an entity containing divine power to accomplish itself.** Thus the judgment word possesses and releases its own power to produce what it proclaims.

■ **The Word of God, once spoken, has a history of its own, it remains alive and powerful in succeeding generations and different situations.**

> *"So is my word that goes out from my mouth:*
> *It will not return to me empty,*
> *but will accomplish what I desire*
> *and achieve the purpose for which I sent it."*
>
> (Isaiah 55:11)

■ **The demons know that every act of disobedience or resistance on their part increases their dread of the Lord who is watching over His word to perform it or to see it fulfilled** (Jeremiah 1:12). When their fear becomes unbearable they give way to the Word of God.

> *"Be quiet!" said Jesus sternly, "Come out of him!" The evil spirit shook the man violently and came out of him with a shriek."*   (Mark 1:25–26)

The effect of authority

We need to distinguish very carefully between power (*dunamis*) and authority (*exousia*).

■ *Power* is the strength or potency to get done whatever you will to do even in the face of opposition or dysfunctional circumstances. In this sense, all power belongs to God.

> *"Once God has spoken*
> *Twice I have heard this:*
> *That power belongs to God."*   (Psalm 62:11, NASB)

■ *Authority* is the delegated right to exercise the prerogatives of power or to represent the power of one whose will and commands must be obeyed by others.

Authority stands in relation to power in much the same way as law stands in relation to the state with its police and its armed forces. Authority acts on behalf of power, but it seeks and expects to obtain the desired results without having to call on the use of coercive power. In the ultimate, however, we obey authority because we recognize that either:

☐ The authority figure also has the power to enforce obedience or punish disobedience, or

☐ It can call on the source of its authority and that power source will enforce obedience to the authority or punish disobedience.

Therefore:

☐ *Authority exercises the right or power to command.*

☐ *Power enforces the commands of authority.*

The authority of the believer and the demons

The distinction between power and authority is important for understanding the authority of the believer over the demons. *Sometimes* the believer is meant **to move in power**, but *always* he is meant **to move in authority**.

The authority of the believer to represent the power of God in relation to Satan and the demons is dependent on the following conditions:

■   *Obedience.* The believer must be living in obedience to the source of his power, that is, to Christ. Like the Roman centurion who so impressed Jesus, he must be a man "under authority".

> *"But just say the word, and my servant will be healed. For I myself am a man under authority, with soldiers under me. I tell this one, 'Go,' and he goes; and that one, 'Come,' and he comes, I say to my servant, 'Do this,' and he does it."*
>
> (Matthew 8:8–9)

The centurion's men obeyed him without question because they knew that if they disobeyed the centurion, the centurion's superior officer would back him up and *his* superior officer would back him up, all the way back to Caesar on his throne in Rome. All the power of the Roman Empire stood behind the centurion-as long as he stayed under authority. If he stepped out of that obedience he would have no authority at all.

The authority of the believer therefore depends on two factors:

1. The power and authority that belongs to Christ as Head of the Church.

2. Our relationship to Christ, and that relationship is obedience.

■ *A knowledge of the extent of his authority*, that is, what he can do and command and what things are beyond the scope of his rights in this regard.

The authority of Christ is absolute, all authority in heaven and on earth, spiritual and temporal (Matthew 28:18). As Head of the Church He has delegated authority to His Body:

☐ Over sickness and demons

> *"He . . . gave them authority over unclean spirits, to cast them out, and to heal every disease and every infirmity."*
>
> (Matthew 10:1, RSV)

☐ Over all of Satan's ability

> *"Behold, I have given you authority to tread upon serpents and scorpions, and over all the power of the enemy; and nothing shall hurt you."* (Luke 10:19, RSV)

Of one thing you can be certain, the demons know whether we are sure of our grounds or unsure, and whether we are within the scope of our rightful authority or have exceeded it.

■ *A growing knowledge of the character and the ways and purposes of God* who is the source of his authority.

What gave Jesus such authority on earth was His total identification with the will and purposes of His Father in heaven.

> *"My Father is always at his work to this very day, and I, too, am working."* (John 5:17)

> *"The Son can do nothing by himself; he can do only what he sees his Father doing, because whatever the Father does, the Son also does."* (John 5:19)

"I do nothing on my own but speak just what the Father has taught me. The one who sent me is with me; he has not left me alone, for I always do what pleases him."   (John 8:28–29)

Just as the Father sent the Son into the world to live and act on His behalf, to do His will on earth as it is done in heaven, so Christ has sent us.

"As you sent me into the world, I have sent them into the world."   (John 17:18)

We are to do the same as Jesus did, to do the will of the One who has sent us, that is, to do on earth the things that are in harmony with His deeds in heaven.

It is for this reason that Scripture has given us such a mass of information on the way in which Jesus lived and thought and acted. His life is told four times over in the Gospels, one third of the entire New Testament. We need a continuous and continual revelation of His character and His works, the "seeing" that Jesus spoke about in John 5:19.

■ **Confidence to act on His authority**. This is the critical point because authority is not authority unless it is used. If we know our grounds and know the kind of decisions and responses that are appropriate, then we have to act. Specifically we need:

☐ Confidence to act or decide, or command.

☐ Confidence in the decisions we make or the commands we give, and

☐ Confidence that Christ will back us up and, if necessary, enforce our commands or decisions.

It is here that **our will becomes important**. In binding the activity of the demons, or releasing their hold on people, we have to hold the commands we give in the name or authority of Christ, with our will against the will of the demons. And we have to hold that pressure against them until resistance crumbles. God's will is done by God willing it in heaven and man willing it on earth, actively insisting at all costs, *"Thy will be done on earth as it is in heaven."*

In other words, **the force of authority is moral pressure**. The person exercising it makes the other person feel uneasy and threatened if they resist so that eventually they give way in order to get release from the pressure. That is the pressure that commands truly given in the authority of Jesus Christ put on the demons.

The pressure is increased when the person exercising authority is **confident of their position and confident of the final outcome of the conflict** and the person resisting is unsure of themselves and of their ability to successfully resist.

The Prussian General, Clauswitz, wrote in his principles of warfare that it is more important to destroy the courage of the enemy's troops than to destroy his troops. The same principles hold true in spiritual warfare. Praise, worship, the proclamation of Scripture and the rehearsing of the works of God not only encourage our confidence in victory, they devastate the morale and will to resist of the evil spirits.

Authority and the Name of Jesus

Authority is vested in the Name of Jesus.

> *"God exalted him to the highest place*
> *and gave him the name that is above every name,*
> *that at the name of Jesus every knee should bow,*
> *in heaven and on earth and under the earth,*
> *and every tongue confess that Jesus Christ is Lord,*
> *to the glory of God the Father.*

(Philippians 2:9–11)

Authority is in the Name, power is in the Spirit. When the disciples were sent out by Jesus and given authority over the demons, they reported, *"Lord, even the demons submit to us in your name."* The signs that were promised to accompany those who believe were:

> *"In my name they will drive out demons; they will speak in new tongues; they will pick up snakes with their hands; and when they drink deadly poison, it will not hurt them at all; they will place their hands on sick people, and they will get well."*   (Mark 16:17–18)

The Name of Jesus sums up all He is in His victory, His standing, His office as Prophet, Priest and King, His exaltation and His eternal glory. All authority in heaven and on earth has been given to Him (Matthew 28:18). When we speak or act in His Name, we represent Him, therefore we are to do the works that He did, in the same spirit that He did and with the same end, to glorify the Father.

Christ has unlimited authority, even infinite authority. We do not have authority to that extent, but to the extent that He has given us authority we are to use it, not to say but to do. It is not a matter of merely saying, "In the Name of Jesus", it is seeing that God's will is done on earth as it is in heaven by:

☐ **Understanding** His will, both the general and the specific

☐ **Obeying** His will

☐ **Embodying** His will, and

☐ **Doing** His will, that is, *willing* His will.

The will of the believer, humbly and obediently resting in the divine will, and actively willing that will against the powers of darkness is what puts demons to flight. Their fear is, that if they resist too long they will face the power of a holy God who will come to enforce the commands of His servants.

It is to the power aspect of binding and loosing that we will turn in the next chapter.

The Power of the Holy Spirit

We have seen that authority rests on power, and that authority without the power to back up its commands is helpless. On the other hand, where authority is accompanied by access to adequate power it need not necessarily use that power. It is capable of producing results solely by the moral weight and influence that power gives to its commands.

As far as the authority of the believer is concerned, including that of binding and loosing, the power that backs up and validates that authority is the power of the Holy Spirit. He is the One who dwells in us (1 Corinthians 3:16), and has made us competent as ministers of the new covenant (2 Corinthians 3:6). The power gifts that are meant to mark the ministry of the Church are manifestations of His presence (1 Corinthians 12:4–10). We still have to ask, however:

☐ What is meant by the power of the Holy Spirit?

☐ What kind of power is it?

☐ How are we meant to gain access to that power?

The Holy Spirit and power

Spirit and power are linked together with unfailing regularity throughout the whole of Scripture, and particularly when we turn to the Gospel record of the life of Jesus.

He was conceived when the power of the Spirit over-shadowed the Virgin Mary (Luke 1:35) and His public ministry began when the Holy Spirit came upon Him after His baptism (Mark 1:10). He was sent by the Spirit into the desert to face the strong man, Satan (Mark 1:12–13) and returned from that victory in the power of the Spirit (Luke 4:14).

It was the Holy Spirit whose anointing consecrated Jesus as the Messiah, the Lord's Anointed King, and who empowered Him to preach good news to the poor, freedom for prisoners and release for the oppressed (Luke 4:18). Henceforth everything He did, He did as a man filled with the Holy Spirit. He healed by the power of the Holy Spirit (Acts 10:38), and when He cast out demons He did it by the Spirit of God (Matthew 12:28).

After the resurrection, the disciples also were told to wait in the city until they were *"clothed with power from on high"* (Luke 24:49) and that they would receive that power when the Holy Spirit came upon them (Acts 1:8). Throughout the history of the early Church the same linking of Spirit and power is maintained. When the gathered church prayed for God to stretch out His hand to heal and to perform miraculous signs and wonders, the place where they were meeting was shaken and they were all filled with the Holy Spirit (Acts 4:30–31).

Henceforth the apostolic preaching is not simply with words, but also with power, with the Holy Spirit (1 Thessalonians 1:5), and signs and miracles represent the demonstration of the Spirit's power (Romans 15:19; 1 Corinthians 2:5).

The nature of the Spirit's power

The Greek word for power, *dunamis*, is the root of our English word "dynamite", but the power of the Holy Spirit is not to be thought of in those terms. It is not some kind of energy flow or force field.

The Holy Spirit who is the power of the Lord, is a person, therefore His power is the power of personal presence.

Where the Holy Spirit is, the power of the Lord is present, and where the power of the Lord is manifested, it is because the Holy Spirit is present.

Note the following important points:

■ *The presence of God is not the same on every occasion or in every place*. Firstly, there is a structural or general presence of the Holy Spirit in creation.

> *"In him we live and move and have our being."*
>
> (Acts 17:28)

> *"Where can I go from your Spirit?*
> *Where can I flee from your presence?*
> *If I go up to the heavens, you are there;*
> *if I make my bed in the depths,*
> *you are there.*
> *If I rise on the wings of the dawn,*
> *if I settle on the far side of the sea,*
> *even there your hand will guide me,*
> *your right hand will hold me fast."*
>
> (Psalm 139:7–10)

This structural presence of God undergirds all forms of more specific manifestations of His presence amongst His people.

■ *Secondly, the Holy Spirit is especially present at certain times, and especially present in certain places*. These occasions are to be understood as a greater intensification of His presence. Even in the ministry of Jesus such experiences of the manifestation of the Holy Spirit's presence seem to have been variable. For example, the Holy Spirit who came upon Him as a dove at His baptism, was also the cloud that enveloped Him on the Mount of Transfiguration (Mark 9:7). He was the power of the Lord that was present for Jesus to perform healing (Luke 5:17), and that was coming from Him and healing those who touched Him (Luke 6:19; 8:46). These occasions are specially noted, but Jesus, who had the Spirit without measure, always moved in authority, whether the specific manifestation of the Spirit's presence was observable or not.

■ *Our experience of the Holy Spirit's presence will follow that of Jesus.* The Spirit is the anointing that we have received, and He abides (1 John 2:27), because we are indwelt by His presence (1 Corinthians 3:16). But we will experience the power of the Holy Spirit in a special measure from time to time. On those occasions there is an intensified presence of the Spirit within us or amongst us. In different terminology it is the difference between being full of the Holy Spirit which is meant to be our continual experience (Luke 4:1) and being filled with the Spirit for a particular purpose (Acts 4:8).

■ The nature of the Holy Spirit's power, as that of personal presence, also governs its character. Thus He is:

☐ *The Spirit of glory* (1 Peter 4:14). Glory is God's majesty and power, and power and glory interpenetrate one another (Ephesians 3:16; Colossians 1:11; Revelation 15:8).

☐ *The Spirit of holiness* (Romans 1:4). Holiness is God's unique dignity, He alone is holy (1 Samuel 2:2). *"Holy and awesome is his name"* (Psalm 111:9).

☐ *The Spirit of love* (Romans 5:5) who unites, us to Himself so that nothing will ever separate us from the love of Christ (Romans 8:38–39) and intercedes for us *"with groans that words cannot express"* (Romans 8:26*)*.

☐ *The Spirit of grace* (Hebrews 10:29) expressed in forgiveness, kindness, acceptance and magnanimity towards the undeserving.

☐ *The Spirit of life* (Romans 8:2) – creative, redemptive and death swallowing.

All these, and many other manifestations of the Spirit's power constitute the moral and spiritual splendor of God's presence that will overthrow Satan and all his hosts (2 Thessalonians 2:8) because no evil can stand before His holiness. In Jesus' person it caused the demons to cry out in fear *"What have you to do with us, O Son of God? Have you come here to torment us before the time?"* (Matthew 8:29, RSV).

How do we gain access to the Holy Spirit's power?

Because the power of the Holy Spirit is the power of personal presence, we are dealing with those special intensifications of His presence that seem to take place at particular times and on particular occasions. Regarding them we can make the following observations:

■ *The intensification of the Holy Spirit's presence can be affected by the part played by man.*

☐ It is adversely affected by man's sin and rebellion (Psalm 51:11; Isaiah 63:10; Jeremiah 23:39). God has given up the use of coercive power to protect the integrity of the relationship He desires with man.

☐ It is positively affected by human receptivity and human need (Isaiah 61:1ff.; Acts 10:44), and the openness of the situation.

■ *We are able to experience such intensifications of the Holy Spirit's presence*, but not to produce them. Nevertheless we can, and should ask for them and seek them (Exodus 33:15; Acts 4:29–31).

■ *The intensifications of divine presence seem to have these characteristics*:

☐ They are temporary,

☐ They are initiated by God, that is there is a certain sovereignty about them (Joel 2:28), and,

☐ They are effective (Romans 15:18–19).

Nevertheless there remains the possibility of disbelief or rejection, they do not compel faith (Matthew 12:38–39).

Openness to the Holy Spirit's presence

Although there is a sovereignty about the special intensifications of the Holy Spirit's presence, it is His desire to be present in such ways with us. The openness and receptivity that can enable Him to be present amongst us is developed in the following ways:

■ *Through the baptism in the Holy Spirit*. Power, which means presence, is the promised result of the baptism in the Holy Spirit (Acts 1:8; 2:1–4, etc.). The Holy Spirit is the Angel or Messenger of God's Presence (Isaiah 63:11).

■ *Through the operation of the gifts of the Holy Spirit* (1 Corinthians 12:7–10). The gifts are described as manifestations of the

Spirit, that is, personal communications by Him or special enablings or capacities bestowed by His intensified presence in us.

■ *Through prayer and intercession.* Prayer in the life of Jesus was the key to His experience of the Spirit's presence and power (cf. Luke 6:12 with Luke 6:19). Intercession by the church in Acts 4:23–31 was answered by a dramatic experience of the Holy Spirit's presence.

■ *Through praise and worship.* Like intercession, worship opens up our lives to the divine presence. He inhabits the praises of Israel (Psalm 22:3 margin, ASB).

■ *Through an attitude of expectancy.* Receptivity to the presence of the Holy Spirit must be cultivated as a continual attitude of heart. God answers our expectations, and none more so than the Holy Spirit who dwells in our body as His temple. The Holy Spirit is no less than God localized in us, seeking our fellowship and our communion. Note the importance of praying in the Spirit (1 Corinthians 14:2, 14–15; Jude 20).

The importance of the Holy Spirit in binding and loosing

All that we have dealt with in this study arises from God's intention to share His power with mankind so that man can cooperate with Him in achieving His goals for creation. But through the Fall, man has been set on a course of misusing the power given to him and with the existence of Satan and the evil spirits there is a power clash in the universe.

Nevertheless, for the sake of the integrity of the relationship God desires with man, He has laid aside the use of coercive power; His power is with man and for man rather than control over man. His intention is unchanged, that redeemed man should effect His will on earth as it is done in heaven. His presence and His power are to enable this to be done by working with man and through man.

The intensified presence of the Holy Spirit is of vital importance for the exercise of our authority to bind and loose, in the following ways:

■ *To give us revelation as to the extent of our authority and what has been given us.*

> *"We have not received the spirit of the world but the Spirit who is from God, that we might understand what God has freely given us."*   (1 Corinthians 2:12)

■ *To give us revelation regarding the character and ways and purposes of God.*

> *"For who among men knows the thoughts of a man except the man's spirit within him? In the same way no-one knows the thoughts of God except the Spirit of God."*
>
> (1 Corinthians 2:11)

■ *To give us discernment and knowledge as to the nature of the demonic strong man or strongholds we are facing.* This may come through the spiritual gifts of a word of knowledge, a word of wisdom, or the discerning of spirits.

■ *To guide us in the use of Scripture*, the *"sword of the Spirit"* against the demons (Ephesians 6:17), particularly the *rhema* word, the specific Spirit-quickened word.

■ *For the gift of miracles to effect deliverance and the gift of healings* if necessary, where the word of authority does not produce a decisive result, to bind up any damage that the person has suffered.

■ *That we ourselves may be continuously strengthened in the inner man* (Ephesians 3:16) so as not to be affected by the battle.

SECTION 3

Defensive Spiritual Warfare

Introduction

The issue of defensive spiritual warfare is one of the most exciting yet crucial issues that faces the Church today.

There are a number of Christians and churches who are going through very difficult times in these days. They have got hold of the idea of spiritual warfare, galloped into battle, and then been suddenly flattened and they don't know why. I believe the reason is they have not learned how to defend themselves in a war. It is something they don't understand.

The psalmist says that it is God *"who trains my hands for war, my fingers for battle"* (Psalm 144:1). God trains us for battle. If we get into spiritual warfare and we are untrained in the principles and issues facing us, we will be flattened if we are not careful.

So this section deals with the whole issue of how spiritual warfare impacts our personal and corporate life, and what is involved in defending them.

Recognizing a Spiritual Attack

I want to start by making the point that in the troubles and difficulties we go through from time to time as Christians, we need to distinguish very carefully what is a spiritual attack from:

■ *The inevitable consequences that follow from our disobedience or our violation of the principles of Scripture.*

We have to be careful not to expect demons to "pop out of the woodwork" every time we come against something difficult in our lives, or we will always be telling people we are under attack and having such a terrible time! You may be – or you may not be, for to be honest, one of the reasons we often face problems as Christians, is because we are actually violating God's principles, or neglecting the instruction of God's Word. If you don't behave correctly in those areas then your Christian life is going to come unstuck, so it won't be spiritual warfare at all.

In fact the devil does not need to bother with us when that happens. I think that one of the things the devil does is to tempt Christians so that when we fall, when we disobey God by neglecting His principles, Satan can just walk off and leave us to carry the consequences of our misdeeds. That is not spiritual warfare.

■ **The circumstances that are permitted by the Holy Spirit as character building exercises or growth lessons in faith.**
There are certain difficult circumstances that we go through that are actually meant to be training exercises. God wants them to produce character in us. They are meant to produce some stamina and backbone in our Christian life. I would encourage you, particularly those who would claim to be charismatic Christians, to spend quite a bit of time reading Paul's second letter to the church at Corinth. When you do, you will be surprised to find that Paul says things like this: *"I was depressed . . . I was scared . . . I was afraid . . . I was so pressured I thought I was going to die."* This was Paul, the great and mighty apostle. It amazes me how frank Paul is with the stresses he goes through as a believer.

When we go through those stresses, we need to understand God's purpose is that they are meant to be training exercises for us. I used to preach a message called "The Gospel of Suffering" but people today don't want to listen to "The Gospel of Suffering", so I called it "Biblical Stress Management"! It's the same thing.

The church that Paul wrote to so frankly wasn't the magisterial church of Rome; it wasn't his favorite church of Philippi; it wasn't the wonderful revelational church of Ephesus; it was the church at Corinth. That bunch of crazy charismatics that took Paul all his time to keep on track! This was the church he opened his mind to about his problems. He understood it was not spiritual warfare.

Summary

We must distinguish what is really spiritual attack from either:

☐ The inevitable consequences that follow our disobedience or our violation of the principles of Scripture, or

☐ The circumstances that are permitted by the Holy Spirit as character building exercises or growth lessons in faith.

Why Christians Come Under Spiritual Attack

Spiritual warfare, or attack, is liable to happen to us in the following circumstances. It is important that we understand why.

1. We are a threat to the devil's position or his possessions

If in our life, in our faith, or in our behavior individually or corporately the devil thinks that we are threatening his possessions or his position, he will attack. He has learned that the best means of defense is attack and so he will react. Those of you in business are, I am sure, often aware of what I mean. I want you to understand what happens.

A business or a corporation or a city, or for that matter a church, has an inner life that is actually spirit. We are spirit beings and when we corporately create an organization there comes into being a corporate spirit. This thing is alive. This thing manages people, uses people, shapes people, controls people and dominates people. I remember speaking at a business seminar in Oxford, England, and a man came up to me afterwards and said, "I am a senior manager in an oil company and what you are saying today is exactly right. I have to go to meetings of people from all different oil companies. I can walk into a room and within five minutes, without anybody telling me the company they belong to, I can pick them every time. They talk differently, their attitudes are different, they behave differently. They are stamped by their company life." When we are serving the business, serving the government department or whatever, we are aware of that.

This "corporate spirit" is not only alive but it is fallen. It is not only fallen but it is idolatrous, and it has two main aims.

■ *It will do anything to survive.* Many years ago in New Zealand, I remember seeing an interview on television with the then Prime Minister. The interviewer said to him, "Mr Prime Minister, what is the first principle of government?" Now you would think he would have said that the first principle of government is to govern, or the first principle of government is justice but he didn't say that. He said, "The first principle of government is to stay in power." He would do anything to survive. A church will do anything to survive. A business will do anything to survive.

■ *The second thrust of a corporation is idolatry.* In Isaiah 47:8 Babylon the City says this:

> "*I am, and there is none besides me.*
> *I will never be a widow*
>   *or suffer the loss of children.*"

In contrast in Isaiah 45:18, 21 God says:

> "*I am . . .*
> *And there is no God apart from me.*"

The corporation has this idolatrous drive that it wants to dominate people and be the ultimate authority of their lives.

I remember a man at that same seminar who said to me, "Last week I was at church during the week and my boss rang up. My wife said, 'Bill's not here but at a church meeting' and down the telephone came an annoyed voice saying, 'What on earth is he doing at a church meeting? I want him at home doing his paperwork. He has got to be on the road in the morning.'"

What does that show? It shows an idolatrous drive in the business spirit that wants to rule. Whenever a Christian lives under a corporation like that, the corporation tries to impact the shape of the believer's life, and to establish its value standards and its ethical standards. It shows that this is the spirit that the employee has to obey. Sometimes those standards are non-Christian and even anti-Christian as far as you and I are concerned. We are aware of that impact.

We need to understand about the demonic powers whose aim is to manage and control the corporation and what is happening all the time. Some of the decisions made in boardrooms may be totally amoral as far as the Christian is concerned. What is driving those people? They are not necessarily evil men. They are being dominated by demonic powers and the same powers may well be trying to influence believers.

What is our protection? It is this. We are indwelt by the Holy Spirit and His presence in the believer's life can keep us free from that domination by a business power. We can live with the business, like Daniel, serve it legitimately because it can have legitimate ends, and do so without bending the knees, without allowing it to impose its moral standard upon us. But to be realistic we have to understand that if we are doing that, there will be antagonism from the corporation and antagonism from the demons. That is where we are liable to come under spiritual attack.

I have no doubt that many of you reading this will have

been aware of an alien force, a non-Christian influence, in your workplace. You are most likely up against demonic powers. You threaten their position and authority because of the presence of the Holy Spirit within you.

2. Satan is probing for our weaknesses

It can happen to us because all the time the devil is probing for our weaknesses. He believes that every one of us has a place of "battlefield vulnerability". He wants to discover what that is and he will do anything to find it.

The devil believes that every one of us has our price. Every one of us has our breaking point. That is what he is after. This is the cause of much of the pressure we come under from time to time.

3. Satan is trying to neutralize and destroy us

More seriously, if the devil can neutralize us, then he will destroy us. This is his ultimate aim. It is vitally important that we understand that the war we are involved in is a real war. It is not make-believe. We are not playing games. The enemy wants to get us on our own and destroy us so he will try to isolate us: isolate us from God, isolate us from one another, isolate us from our friends, isolate us from our churches. When he has done this and we are on our own, he will seek to destroy us.

It is important to understand that most attacks come through people. Words will be said by people and things will be done by people. Actions will be taken by people. Bitterness will flow from the hearts of people. Remember, however, that people are never the enemy. The important thing to do when these things come upon us is to discern the real source of the attack, what it really is, so that we can deal with it. If you simply react to people you have lost the battle.

Do you remember the time when Jesus was speaking to the disciples and asked them, *"Who do you say I am?"* and Peter said, *"You are the Christ, the Son of the living God."* (Matthew 16:15–16). It seems as if Jesus was so excited about that, He started to tell Peter He was going to go to Jerusalem, He was going to be crucified, He was going to be buried and He was going to rise again from the dead. What happened? Peter went straight up the wall! "That is never going to happen to you," he exclaimed. "Get rid of that, Lord, that's rubbish!" There was pressure on the spirit of Jesus. There was an attack coming at Him. Somehow the enemy was trying to get Him isolated from the Father's will and purpose for His life. Jesus discerned this and strongly rebuked Peter. *"Get behind me, Satan!"* He said (Matthew 16:23). He wasn't having a go at Peter. The words came out of Peter's mouth but they originated from the devil.

We have to realize and remind ourselves all the time that, though people may be the vehicle of the attack, the person is never the enemy, I repeat, never the enemy. This is why sometimes you find that the devil can use Christians to attack other believers.

Summary

We are called to live in the power structures and to serve their legitimate ends but under the Lordship of Christ to refuse to:

☐ Yield to the idolatrous spirit of the powers.

☐ Take our moral standards or value system from the powers, and

☐ Allow the powers to be the ultimate authority in our life.

We must reckon realistically that from time to time we will come under attack from demonic powers.

Spiritual attack is the devil's attempt to deter us individually or corporately from pressing into battle and hitting targets. He understands that the best means of defense is attack.

☐ He believes that we all have our price and our areas of vulnerability.

☐ Satan is probing for our weaknesses.

☐ The attacks can show us what weaknesses are sins, which calls for repentance and amendment.

What vulnerabilities call for protective strategies?

Alone or in relationships that we cannot trust we are vulnerable. Satan is trying to:

☐ Isolate us from God and other believers.

☐ Disable our defenses.

Attack will most often come through people, **but remember people are never the enemy**. It takes real discernment to realize the true nature and source of the attack (Matthew 16:21–23).

Sources and Nature of Demonic Attack

In this chapter I want to give you some situations where this kind of spiritual attack can happen. Below is a check-list of circumstances which may occur in your personal life, your family life and your church life which are likely to be spiritual attacks from demonic powers.

Not every example given is necessarily evidence of demonic attack, but we need to recognize they may be.

1. Physical attacks

☐ Sicknesses or physical conditions that have no medical reason or do not respond to medical treatment.

☐ Attacks involving the appetites – eating disorders, food allergies, anorexia, alcoholism or drinking habits.

☐ Sexual appetites, lust, sexual perversion, pornography, sexual disorders.

☐ Nervous weaknesses and disorders, drug addictions.

2. Attacks on the mind

☐ Compulsive or obsessive thoughts.

☐ Ungovernable tongues given to criticism, slander and backbiting.

☐ Confusion in thinking, extreme talkativeness or inability to communicate, extreme forgetfulness, fantasizing, perplexity, overactive imagination.

☐ Bad dreams, nightmares, insomnia or sleeplessness.

☐ Indecision, indecisiveness, excessive procrastination, passivity.

3. Emotional attacks

☐ Fears, worry, anxiety, dread.

☐ Depression, moroseness, negativity.

☐ Discouragement, hopelessness, despair.

☐ Self-doubt, condemnation, sense of failure.

☐ Anger, aggressiveness, hostility, defensiveness.

4. Occult manifestations

☐ Apparitions, visions.

☐ Demonization.

☐ Psychic or mediumistic experiences or manifestations.

☐ Self-destructive or suicidal tendencies.

☐ Effects of curses or maledictions.

5. Attacks based on personal sins

☐ Bitterness, resentments, unforgiveness.

☐ Rebellion against authority.

☐ Pride and self-centeredness.

☐ Unconfessed and secret sins and self-indulgences.

6. Attacks based on generational or ancestral sin

7. Abusive attacks

☐ Domination, intimidation, control.

☐ Sexual, emotional or verbal abuse.

☐ Spiritual, psychological and other forms of abuse.

8. Attacks on marriages and families

☐ Conflict, strife, breakdown in communication.

☐ Sexual problems.

☐ Parent/child behavioral problems.

☐ Adulterous relationships or temptations.

9. Attacks on business and church life

☐ Division and disunity.

☐ Relational conflict, disloyalty, betrayal.

☐ Personal attacks on character, ability, position or rights.

☐ Rumor-mongering, gossip, character assassination.

☐ Injustice, unfair treatment, persecution.

☐ Financial and business pressures, unfair competition and opposition.

☐ Pressure, stress and burn out.

10. Attacks on the spiritual life

☐ Severe and irrational doubt, discouragement, lack of reality.

☐ Resistance to prayer, Scripture and worship.

☐ Deception, imbalance, false manifestations and cultic revelations.

I am not saying that everything I have listed always has a demonic source, but we need to be alert and check the source of the attack if any of the above things are around. It is clear just looking at the list to what extent our life can be interfered with and attacked by demonic powers.

Principles of Defensive Warfare

18

Now I want to give you some of the principles of defensive spiritual warfare for you to think about and study. We cannot over-emphasize the importance of defense, because the lack of secure defense leaves us open to surprise attack. This happens too frequently to Christians.

The devil will often try and rush our defenses and over-whelm us. If our position is not secure, this will happen easily, and we will be bowled over before we know what has happened.

Occupy the high ground

> *"He who dwells in the shelter of the Most High*
> *will rest in the shadow of the Almighty.*
> *I will say of the LORD, 'He is my refuge and my fortress,*
> *my God, in whom I trust.'*
>
> *Surely he will save you from the fowler's snare*
> *and from the deadly pestilence.*
> *He will cover you with his feathers,*
> *and under his wings you will find refuge;*
> *his faithfulness will be your shield and rampart.*

You will not fear the terror of night,
  nor the arrow that flies by day,
nor the pestilence that stalks in the darkness,
  nor the plague that destroys at midday.
A thousand may fall at your side,
  ten thousand at your right hand,
  but it will not come near you.
You will only observe with your eyes
  and see the punishment of the wicked.

If you make the Most High your dwelling –
  even the LORD, *who is my refuge –*
then no harm will befall you,
  no disaster will come near your tent.
For he will command his angels concerning you
  to guard you in all your ways;
they will lift you up in their hands,
  so that you will not strike your foot against a stone.
You will tread upon the lion and the cobra;
  you will trample the great lion and the serpent.

'Because he loves me,' says the LORD, *'I will rescue him;*
  I will protect him, for he acknowledges my name.
He will call upon me, and I will answer him;
  I will be with him in trouble,
  I will deliver him and honour him.
With long life will I satisfy him
  and show him my salvation.' ''

(Psalm 91:1–16)

This is an amazing psalm. David says it all so much better than I can!

The first principle of defensive warfare is to get onto the high ground. This is where you are safe, and where you can see what is happening. Battlefields are very confusing places where there is a lot of noise, a lot of smoke and a lot of things going on, and nobody knows what is happening. The devil will therefore try and get us down on to his ground where this kind of thing can affect us. The first and primary principle, therefore, of all defensive warfare is to get on to the high ground so that you can see what is going on from the beginning. This is where you are in touch with resources that will keep you safe and where your position is protected.

What is the high ground? Spiritually we have the high ground but in the secular city who has the high ground? If you look around the horizon of a city you will see who has! Have you ever wondered why those great gleaming skyscrapers are built – the banks, insurance companies, and multi-national companies? Do you understand that they are making a "spiritual" statement? The Bible is full of references to high places. If you go into a pagan country and look around the hills you will find that the temples are built there on the high ground – they are making a statement. In a city those towers are making a spiritual statement. They are saying, "Here we have the power, here we have the resources, here we call the shots, here you bow to us." Their aim is to over-awe us with their power and cause us to bow the knee to them.

Recently I was in the city of Melbourne in Australia and there is a huge multi-storey office tower block being built right across the end of the main street there. It is the head office of one of the major brewers in the State of Victoria. When it is finished it will be difficult for anyone to go up the main street of that city without being confronted with this office block speaking about their brewery. There is a spiritual statement behind that. In the world the devil occupies the high ground so we need to know what our high ground is.

1. Our high ground is our revelational standing in Jesus Christ

I recommend you to read the psalms of David. He was a man of war and knew the business of warfare. He is always speaking about "the LORD, my rock, my refuge, my high tower, my stronghold, my shield, my rampart." David knew what his high ground was.

> *"I love you, O LORD, my strength.*
>
> *The LORD is my rock, my fortress, and my deliverer;*
>   *my God is my rock, in whom I take refuge.*
> *He is my shield and the horn of my salvation,*
>   *my stronghold.*
> *I call to the LORD who is worthy of praise,*
>   *and I am saved from my enemies."*
>
> (Psalm 18:1–3)

David's psalms are full of these kinds of words. You would think by reading them, however, that he was always running away from his enemies. Not so. Read the history and you will see that David was always running after his enemies! He knew where his stronghold, his safe place, his security was. He knew that the first principle of warfare was to get your defense secure. The first thing you need to know about battle is how to defend yourself before you can learn how to attack the enemy. We need to be trained for battle.

> *"It is God who arms me with strength*
>   *and makes my way perfect.*
> *He makes my feet like the feet of a deer;*
>   *he enables me to stand on the heights.*
> *He trains my hands for battle . . ."*
>
> (Psalm 18:32–34)

God knows that we are in a war so He wants to train us for battle. The first principle of training is to get your defense secure and this is done by firstly knowing what your high ground is and your standing in Christ. **I am seated in**

heavenly places with God in Christ. That is the Christian's security and high ground.

2. Our high ground is the victory of the death of Jesus Christ on the cross

This is what the Bible means by the blood of Christ. The blood of Christ is a shorthand expression that sums up all the power, the awesome power, of the Cross on our behalf. That's our high ground. I am seated in Christ in heavenly places – I am there! I am covered with the blood of Christ. Jesus said before the Cross, *"the ruler of this world is coming, and he has **nothing** in Me"* (John 14:30, NASB; emphasis added) – no ground, no place – **nothing**.

When I plead the blood of Christ, what happens is that what was true about Christ becomes true about me and you. The devil has no ground or place in you – that's our high ground and that's our refuge and our stronghold. Not our own strength, not our own wits, not our own knowledge, not even our own faith. Our high ground is the blood of Christ.

3. Our high ground is our covenantal relationships in the Body of Christ

You and I are part of the Body of Christ. Let me explain how this works. Imagine that you are in a church with many other believers and holding hands along the rows and across the gangways. Now if someone comes into the room and tries to take hold of just one of those believers there, he is going to have a problem. As the intruder tries to pull a person out, so he confronts all the strength of the whole Body there, because all are joined (holding hands) with one another. He is going to have a problem! This simple illustration shows that we are locked into the Body of Christ by covenant, bound into a covenantal relationship with the entire Body of Christ, not just in our local village or town but right across the world. Millions and millions of Christians are involved.

In the past and in the ages to come there is a "great crowd of witnesses". You and I are locked together into that Body. That is our high place – our place of security.

We need to know not only what that high place is, but we also need to know how to get into it. Do you know how to step into that high place within yourself? You must proclaim that, "I am seated in heavenly places in Christ Jesus. My life is hid with Christ in God. I am covered by the blood of the Cross. The devil has nothing in me. I am part of the Body of Christ and Christ is my Head."

You need to know how to step back onto this high ground. You also need to learn to do it before you **have** to do it. This should be part of our daily training because when you need to do it, it may be too late. You get up tomorrow morning feeling fine, rejoicing in God and ready to face another day then suddenly, a short while later, "the sky falls in on your head!" It is too late then to think "I've got the high ground somewhere. What was the high ground? I am sure Tom Marshall told me what it was!"

We need to know beforehand so that we are prepared for the attack. We should practice that – *"God trains our hands for war"*. We must **train** to defend ourselves. On every occasion, under every pressure, through every trial and in everything that happens to us, we have got to know where our high ground is and learn how to get on to it. I think that this should be part of the daily exercise of believers in these days.

Every commanding officer spends an enormous amount of time training troops before he sends them into the trenches! We know that there is a war, but we can't just say, as many Christians do, "Let's go and have a charge at the enemy somewhere." Often we Christians are an untrained bundle of troops thrust into the battlefield in total disarray and we then wonder why we have problems.

When you are occupying the high ground you can see what is going on. You get above the smoke of battle, above the din and above the confusion. One of the things that distinguishes a trainee exercise by the Holy Spirit, and a spiritual attack is clear and obvious. God says, "Face this, go through this, this will be good for you," if you are listening to what He is saying. The mark of a spiritual attack so often is chaos and confusion and you don't understand what is going on. You are attacked from behind – it's bewildering. That is often the mark of a spiritual battle. How are you going to handle that? Get into the high place. From there you can see what is going on much more clearly. You can discern the hand of the devil, the direction of the attack and you can find that place of security – the place of your resources. It is from that place you can say to the devil, "Well I am actually hidden with Christ in God if you want me – I am up here. I am covered by the blood of Christ. If you attack me you actually attack the whole of the Body of Christ because I am part of this Body." You must learn to do this.

Primary rules

■ *With every pressure on your patience, step back into the Body of Christ, into your high place.* Every stress you come under, step back into your high place. Learn to do it, learn to get there, learn to be there. This is a primary rule.

■ *Build an effective defensive system and learn how to defend yourself.* What does this mean?

☐ **Develop an attitude of confidence**. Deal with the question of fear. You need to have a fear-free defense system. Fear saps our morale. Fear confuses us. Fear makes us react in the wrong way. Where is this attitude of confidence to come from? By seeing things the way they really are.

Remember how Elisha was in the town of Dothan one time and the armies of the Assyrians were round the hills outside of the city? Elisha's servant was terrified. What did Elisha do? He asked God to open his eyes. I think Elisha was half humorous about that because he could see things the young fellow couldn't see. The Lord then opened the servant's eyes and he saw:

> *"Those who are with us are more than those who are with them."*   (2 Kings 6:16)

When we see reality, when we see that God is on our side and He is for us, who can be against us?

Do you know what it means that you are filled with the Holy Spirit? The Holy Spirit is God localized in your body. It's a wonderful thought. The Holy Spirit is omnipotent God, omniscient God, eternal God, localized in your human body. This body is the temple of the Holy Spirit. Therefore if God eternal, omnipotent and omniscient is in you, to say that, "He that is for us is more than those that are against us" is the understatement of the century! The Bible also says, that *"greater is he that is in you, than he that is in the world"* (1 John 4:4, AV). We must therefore build our defense system by getting our confidence right.

Confidence is trust that has been proved right so often that you don't need to think about it. David had trusted God so often and proved God so much that he said that *"though war break out against me, even then will I be confident"* (Psalm 27:3, emphasis added).

I find that a lot of Christians today are not confident. They are desperately struggling to trust God and to have more faith. They need to learn to have a place of confidence. Do you know God? God's character never changes. You can be confident in that. God's Word never changes. You can be confident in that as well. Have you ever thought what would happen if you went to the Lord believing one of His promises and you heard him say, "I am sorry, I have changed My mind. It doesn't apply any more." It's unthinkable. God keeps His Word. When God makes a promise to us He limits His Sovereignty for all eternity. God limits His freedom of action for ever. There are some things that God literally cannot do. Why? Because He has promised otherwise. He takes promises very seriously.

Do you know why we may have problems with faith? Basically it is because we are faithless people. We make promises very lightly these days and we break them with very little compunction. Most promises we make have got an unwritten proviso I have discovered. It is this – "as long as I still feel the same," "as long as I discover that I have not made a mistake," "as long as something more important doesn't turn up," "as long as it doesn't cost too much," I promise. Remember that God's promises are not conditional. Once He has promised that's it. If I want to grow in faith I must start taking God's promises seriously. One of the reasons we have difficulty in believing God is because if we take promises lightly, we find it difficult to believe that anybody else, particularly God, will take them seriously.

☐ **Clear away entanglements**. Get rid of things that endanger you spiritually. It is very difficult to fight somebody with your shoelaces tied and with your feet entangled!

The devil tries to entangle us because that inhibits our freedom of action when we come to defending ourselves. Because we are in a war the war has to take priority. I believe that God's people these days have to take this matter seriously and get rid of entanglements.

What do I mean by this? For some people they are relational entanglements. Some relationships you have may be of no help to you and even a potential danger to you – they somehow inhibit your freedom of action. They must go.

Sometimes it is financial entanglements. Freedom of action for many people is severely limited because of these. If possible get free of such. Be rid of them.

Sometimes it is habits – debilitating habits that sap our spiritual energies. Sometimes this is a particular danger for leaders who are involved in so many activities – some of which are none of their business! These just sap energy and distract us from our main task. We need to have a sharp focus as to what God means us to be involved in.

Summary

Note the extreme importance of defense. Lack of secure defenses leave us open to surprise attack.

The devil will often try to rush our defenses and catch us unprepared.

■ *Occupy the high ground* (Psalm 91), where you have protection (verses 1–2), are in touch with resources of divine power (verses 3–7), and can discern what is going on (verse 8).

Note David's reliance on the high ground (Psalm 18:2–3, 16–19; 27:5; 61:2–3). Our high ground is:

☐ Our position and standing in Christ (Ephesians 1:18–23; 2:6; Colossians 3:1–4).

☐ The victory of the Cross and resurrection (Colossians 2:15; Hebrews 2:14; Revelation 12:11).

☐ Our covenant relationship with God (Hebrews 6:17–18).

Satan will always try to draw us off our high ground on to his.

■ *Build an effective defense system before it is needed* (Psalm 144:1; 18:34).

☐ Develop an attitude of confidence (Psalm 27:1–3; Jeremiah 17:7). Deal with fear, be confident in the Cross, be confident in the Holy Spirit, and be confident in the Word of God. God's counsel brings to nothing the purposes of the enemy (Proverbs 21:30–31; Isaiah 8:9–10).

☐ Clear away entanglements that hinder our effectiveness or make us vulnerable. These entanglements may include relationships, finances, debilitating habits or energy-draining thought patterns, complicated and non-productive activities, and issues and situations that are not our business. (Matthew 6:25–34; 2 Corinthians 6:14; 1 Timothy 6:9–10; Hebrews 2:1).

Understanding the Armor of God

19

Ephesians 6:11 tells us to *"put on the full armor of God"*. For a long time that passage never meant a great deal to me. I have friends who religiously get up each day and put on their helmet of salvation, their breastplate and tighten their belt, and get their shield and sword and go off to the office. I tried to imagine that and it wasn't an awful lot of help to me. However, one day I started to understand what the armor of God is. This is very important.

The armor of God is a set of life conditions that God wants to establish in you. And when these are established they enable God to work and they prevent Satan from working. The word *panoplia* meaning "full-armor", is used in the New Testament – once in Ephesians 6 and once in Luke 11 where Jesus is talking about the devil. He says, *"When a strong man, fully armed, guards his own house, his possessions are safe"* (Luke 11:21).

Jesus is saying that God has got a full armor, and the devil has a full armor. What is the latter? It is a set of life conditions that he wants to establish in your life. And when they take root in your life they enable him to work, and they prohibit God from working.

As far as warfare is concerned the life conditions in Ephesians 6 are the critical ones. There are other conditions that are important for your maturity, your growth and so on, but as far as defense is concerned Ephesians 6 names the critical ones. What are they?

God's life conditions

1. Truth

Husbands and wives need to walk in the light with one another, speaking the truth to one another. All the truth. Anything that is hidden from one another is a potential danger.

Brothers and sisters in the Body of Christ need to learn to walk in the light with one another. In the eldership of the church I came from in New Zealand we had come to a very wonderful place of truth-speaking amongst the brethren, to the extent that if one of them said something I knew they meant exactly what those words said. There was no hidden agenda. I could trust them. I could say just what I wanted to say, I didn't have to dress it up in any kind of way or say it obliquely so that they would take the right inference out of it. I could just say it and I knew that they would take it at face value. However, it took us so long and there was so much pain to get to that place, I realized just how little truth-speaking had been going on amongst us. We don't say it the way it is. It sometimes hurts to walk in the truth but truth is a wonderful thing.

Sometimes truth wounds, but this wounding heals very quickly. The safest place to be is in the light. Why? Because the devil hates the light. The devil does not come to the light. Jesus said, *"whoever lives by the truth comes into the light, so that it may be seen plainly that what he has done"* (John 3:21). This means judgment on sin, and on wickedness. Walking in the light is the safest place to be. Get that established in your life.

2. Peace (shalom)

Let me tell you something interesting about peace. Peace to the Hebrews was not the absence of war. Peace to the Hebrews was harmony with your friends and victory over your enemies. Isn't that interesting? That's *shalom*. Now I understand what Paul meant when he said, *"The God of peace [shalom] will soon crush Satan under your feet"* (Romans 16:20). That doesn't sound a very peaceful thing, does it? But it is.

Let God establish harmony in your life with your friends and victory over your enemies, peace with God over your sin, peace with God over His dealings in your life and, more than that, the peace of God that garrisons our hearts and minds.

3. Faith – trust

Let me tell you some important things about trust. Trust is a choice you make. It is a risk you take. There is no such thing as costless, riskless trust. The risk you take is that you let the outcome of some part of your life go out of your hands into somebody else's hands. The risk, therefore, in trusting God is that we let some of the outcome of our lives go out of our control, into His. It doesn't surprise me that we are supposed to trust God but it does surprise me that God trusts us. God lives by the terms of His own relationships. In other words God trusts us and trust is a choice God makes, and trust is a risk God takes. Amazing. God takes risks with us! He lets some of the outcome of His purposes go out of His hands into ours. That's awesome. When Jesus went back to heaven and left all the destiny of His Kingdom in the hands of eleven apostles He actually did not have a backup second "team" waiting in the wings if the first lot failed. He trusted us to preach the Gospel to every creature.

4. Hope – the helmet of salvation

Hope is one of the most neglected virtues in the whole of our Christian calendar. Paul says in 1 Corinthians 13:13:

"And now these three remain: faith, hope and love. But the greatest of these is love."

In my lifetime I have heard hundreds of sermons on love, hundreds of sermons on faith but only two preached on hope – and I preached both! What has happened to hope?

Let me give you a definition of hope – this wonderful thing. In the Bible **hope is the confident expectation of something good**. In other words hope is the openness to receive. You will not experience what you don't receive. If you don't receive the love of God you won't experience it. If you don't receive the blessing of God you won't experience it. Nobody experiences more than they receive but you will not receive more than you are open to. If you are not open to healing you won't receive it. If you are not open to encouragement you won't receive it. God's problem is not in the giving because it is His nature to give. God's problem is getting us to receive, and hope is the openness to receive.

We ought to be the most open people on the face of the earth. Do you know what despair is in the Bible? A despairing person is a person whose future has closed in on themselves. No way out – that's despair. No future. Hope, however, is the opposite. All Christians ought to be "open" people, open to God, open to one another, open to life, open to everything apart from sin. Hope is wonderful.

The devil's life conditions are the reverse of God's life conditions:

☐ The armor of God is truth – the devil's is deception and lies.

☐ The armor of God is peace – the devil's is strife and contention.

☐ The armor of God is hope – the devils is despair and depression.

☐ The armor of God is faith – the devil's is mistrust and suspicion.

We need to understand and take on board the life conditions that God wants to establish in us and work on them every day. Why? Because once they are established they become our armor. They become our protection. Understand the armor of God.

Summary

The armor of God is a set of **life conditions** God wants to establish in our life, to enable Him to work, and to prevent Satan from working (cf. Luke 11:21).

■ *Truth* – the effect of truth is to expose lies and so protect us from the devil's deception (John 3:19–20; 2 Corinthians 6:7; Ephesians 6:14).

■ *Righteousness* – our covenant relationship with God through Christ that guarantees safety and ensures victory (Isaiah 59:17; 2 Corinthians 6:7).

■ *Peace* (*shalom*) – harmony with our friends and victory over our enemies (Romans 16:20). Not only peace with God but the peace of God to guard our hearts and minds (Philippians 4:7; Colossians 3:15).

■ *Faith*. The creative link that enables God's power to be shared with man (Ephesians 6:16; 1 John 5:4).

■ *Hope* – the confident expectation of something good; the openness to receive (Hosea 2:15).

■ *Love* – that not only links us to the life of God but is the life of God (2 Corinthians 6:6; 1 John 5:2–5).

■ *The Word of God* – the *rhema*, revelatory word through the Spirit (Ephesians 6:17; Hebrews 1:3; 1 Peter 1:25).

■ *Prayer in the Spirit* (Ephesians 6:18; Jude 20).

CHAPTER

Examine Your Resources

It is vital for all of us in the battle to examine our resources and to know what they are. Do you know what yours are?

1. Your resources are your strengths, the things you do well

Be honest. Spiritually, what are the things that you do really well? If you say you do nothing really well, that is the devil lying to you. What are you good at? For example, I am good at praising God when I am feeling gloomy – that's a strength. I can believe God for healing my body – that's a strength. I can encourage people who are down – that's a strength.

Understand that God has given you two sets of things. Firstly, strengths, gifts and things you are good at doing. Secondly, limitations. Limitations are in your life to make room for other people. If you had all the strengths you need, you wouldn't need anybody else. You would be self-sufficient. God has made you with limitations.

Because of our fallenness we also have weaknesses. Weaknesses you can overcome and you are supposed to overcome, but limitations you will never overcome. God made you with these to be good at some things but not good at everything. The limitations in your life make room for other people and your strengths help somebody else's limitations. Remember, however, that you must know what your strengths are and use them as part of your resources.

2. Your resources are the Body of Christ

Let me point something out to you and explain what I mean. Think of a church with, say, three hundred people in the congregation. Probably over half of these have been Christians for more than ten years, a quarter for more than fve years and the rest, say, about two years. If you look at this as an average it would be fair to guess at this being about seven years. Now with a congregation of this size you therefore have access to approximately 2,100 years of spiritual experience! It is therefore unlikely that you would come across many circumstances in life that had not been faced and overcome by someone in this congregation. These are your resources to call upon. You should be able to find at least one person that has suffered or gone through a trial similar to yours within that congregation.

3. Your resources are the relationships you can depend on

They too are our strengths. People who are living in friendship and covenant with you are those that you should be able to ring up at any time of the day or night to ask them to pray with or for you. If you have a problem you can call on them and they will be sure to help. If I am facing trouble or attack from a situation they will stand with me. Those are my important relationships and those are my resources in the Body of Christ.

It is vitally important to have these and to have people who are loyal to us and to whom we can be loyal. Do you know what loyalty is?

Loyalty says, "I will be with you in the bad times as well as the good." We talk about a fairweather friend – that's a "friend" who is only there in the good times. Our true friends are there in the bad times as well.

Loyalty says, "I will be for you even if everybody else is against you."

Loyalty says, "I will defend you even at risk or cost to myself."

We need loyal friends. We need relationships that will stand the strain, and stand extraordinary strain if need be. Such people are to be prized almost above anything else. A proverb says, *"a brother is born for adversity"* (Proverbs 17:17). Friends are born for adversity, to stick with you through thick and thin. Such friends are much rarer than they ought to be.

I remember a friend of mine in America who grew up amongst the street gangs in his younger days. He said to me once that if he was in a real tight spot he would rather have some of the guys out of the gang at his back than some of his ministerial colleagues! They would run for cover, but that gang was dependable.

You not only need loyal friends but you also need to know who they are. This friendship has to be cultivated before it is needed. You need to know how much strain your friendship will take because if you overload a relationship with more than it can take you will probably damage both friendship and friend.

Summary

■ *Examine your resources*
You cannot fight in someone else's armor (1 Samuel 17:38–40). Assess your personal life and experience to discover:

☐ **Your spiritual strengths** – the things you do well. Your perseverance, patience, hopefulness, good response to pressure, discernment, etc.

☐ **The things you really know** – have confidence in what you know, in revelation truth and what you have proved in your experience, the *rhema* word.

☐ **Relationships you can depend on in difficult times**, and those you trust and can work effectively with.

☐ **The Body of Christ** – the faith, experience and knowledge available in the Christian community you belong to.

Learn to Handle Spiritual Pressure

21

We all know that we have to live in a real world where there are real anxieties and real stresses. All of us are regularly under stress of one kind or another. So often we can sing victory songs in church, but how do you feel the next morning when you go to work? Be honest. I expect that you feel totally powerless for most of the time. Isn't that right?

We need to understand that God knows all about that. We are in fact to find our destiny on the battlefield. The battlefield is for our good. He is maturing the saints through the pain barrier.

I remember some time ago speaking to a young woman who was telling me how she had just finished her first marathon race. She had run 42 kilometers. She explained to me that when you are running a marathon, around the 24 kilometer mark you hit what is called the pain barrier. When you hit this one of two things happen. Either you body gives up and you die by the side of the road, or you struggle through the pain and you know that even if you don't win, you are somehow going to finish the race. Now when she said that, I realized that all around our lives there are these pain barriers. Not all the unpleasant stressful things that happen to us are bad for us. Most of them are actually necessary to us. They are, if you like, growing pains. For example, you cannot grow physically without hitting the pain barrier. If you want to strengthen your arms you lift weights until your arms are ready to drop – then you start lifting more weights! Or you may want to develop stamina, so you go jogging, and just when you are about to collapse – you jog some more!

You can't grow intellectually without the pain barrier. Everybody who has studied understands that. It hurts to concentrate and try and understand enough to take notes and then it hurts to try and remember what you are meant to have learned! It's a pain barrier.

You can't grow relationally without the pain barrier. You hurt people and they hurt you. It hurts to apologize and ask for forgiveness and then start all over again.

You can't grow spiritually without the pain barrier. One of the interesting things about God is that He is very honest. He never says, "This is going to hurt Me more than it hurts you." He says, "This is going to hurt you," but afterwards, if you are exercised by it, you get the peaceful fruits of righteousness.

What I want to emphasize is that you can't ever avoid pain. If you don't get the pain of exercise you get the pain of a sick body. If you don't go through the pain of study you get the pain of ignorance. If you don't go through the pain of relationships you get the pain of loneliness. You can't avoid pain so you might as well make it productive.

Some of the pain and struggle that we go through in our lives are part of the exercise that the Holy Spirit is putting in our way to build spiritual stamina and muscle into us.

But not all pain is of that kind. Sometimes it will be an attack by the devil on your position, on your life, and on your health, and we need to know how to handle that. There will be the day when all of us find ourselves in the middle of a war that is not of our making. It was here before ever you and I were on the scene. It is a real war. It is not a metaphorical war. It is not a make-believe war. It is the aim of Satan to separate God from His creation Word. Do you know what His

Learn to Handle Spiritual Pressure   183

creation Word is? It is two things. Firstly God said, *"Let us make man in our image, after our likeness; and let them have dominion"* (Genesis 1:26, RSV). That is God's declared purpose. Secondly He said, *"The earth will be filled with the knowledge of the glory of the* LORD, *as the waters cover the sea"* (Habakkuk 2:14). Satan's attempt is to separate God from that Word.

Use every experience of spiritual pressure as a learning process. Under pressure always fall back onto what you know. What you know is your armor. You can't fall back onto somebody else's knowledge. You can't fight wearing somebody else's armor – David discovered that with Saul before tackling Goliath! You can only fight in your own armor. Your armor is what you know.

Under pressure we always retreat to what we know and the greater the pressure is the more fundamental becomes that retreat. I say this because I can remember a time in my life when I had my back spiritually right up "against a wall". All that I was left with was this statement of just three words from Psalm 23 – *"The Lord Is!"* Wonderful! **The Lord Is**. That saved me. That saved my sanity. Everything else had gone but I fell back into the refuge, into the strong tower. Nothing could change the fact that **The Lord Is**.

The more pressure there is, the more basic will be the thing you fall back onto. You go back beyond your faith. Paul lived through enormously difficult circumstances but he dug himself right down to that bedrock. Paul knew that. He was who he was, where he was, because ultimately God had purposed it. He knew the *"plan of him who works out everything in conformity with the purpose of his will"* (Ephesians 1:11). That is the fundamental thing – that's the ultimate thing.

Learn how to handle spiritual pressure in every circumstance. Remember you have got to train and practice defense until it becomes instinctive. Don't think, "I can't manage this." No, use the circumstance as an exercise to step back into the high place. Do this until it becomes habitual, until the instinctive thing under any pressure is to go back onto the high ground and to your place of security. It is when you learn to do this that you can handle situations of attack from the devil.

I believe that what I have endeavored to convey to you will be of fundamental importance to Christians in the days to come.

Defense is only the preliminary. In this booklet I have emphasized that you have got to first learn to defend yourself before you can attack. So many Christians get this the wrong way round and are surprised when they meet defeat.

Finally you will see that in Psalm 18:28 it says:

> *"You, O LORD, keep my lamp burning;*
> *my God turns my darkness into light."*

David was in his high place seeing what was going on, and continues:

> *"With your help I can advance against a troop;*
> *with my God I can scale a wall."*
>
> (Psalm 18:29)

From your defense, you can now mount an offense.

Summary

Spiritual pressure rarely sends advance warnings, so we need to know the nature of our high ground and how to reach it. We need to understand the different pains and stresses in our life; and how to fall back instinctively and automatically into a secure place without having to stop and think about it. Our defense must become second nature to us, and we must use every occasion to practice it.

CHAPTER 2

In Conclusion

■ *Identify the true source of the attack*
People are never the enemy, although the attack may often come through people (Matthew 16:23; Ephesians 6:12).

■ *Discern the nature of the attack and the devil's strategy*

☐ It will generally be directed towards an area of weakness (Ephesians 4:27), or an area of ignorance (2 Corinthians 2:10–11).

☐ Watch out for any negative, compulsive reactions and responses, and shut them down. Our victory is in Christ, but preparation and composure are our responsibility.

■ *Be confident*
You cannot win with a loser's expectancy, or if you feel "unworthy". The principle of victory is still *"according to your faith be it unto you"*. Resolve that you will not quit but will win (Romans 8:37). We are more than conquerors.

■ *Stand fast and resist the attack*

☐ It takes energy for demons to attack. A simple resolute refusal to yield based on our position in Christ, will sap the enemy's strength.

☐   When we stand fast, what the devil dreads is the possibility of Christ's intervention on our behalf (James 4:7–8; 1 Peter 5:8–10).

☐   Attack the devil's attack, and make use of intercession to thwart the enemy's plans (Psalm 33:10; Isaiah 8:7–11), praise and worship to confound his powers (2 Chronicles 20:21; Psalm 149:6), and the prophetic Scriptures to bind the enemy (Matthew 16:19; Revelation 12:11).

■ *Recognize the occasions when confrontation may not be the right thing to do*
There are times when it is wise to duck (1 Samuel 18:7–11).

> *"A man's wisdom gives him patience;*
> *it is to his glory to overlook an offence."*
>
>   (Proverbs 19:11)

On occasions when we are not ready or we don't know what to do or how to handle the situation, the best thing to do might be to withdraw or run away.

> *"The name of the LORD is a strong tower;*
> *the righteous run to it and are safe."*
>
>   (Proverbs 18:10)

If you have enjoyed this book and would like to help us to send a copy of it and many other titles to needy pastors in developing nations, please write for further information or send your gift to:

Sovereign World Trust
PO Box 777, Tonbridge
Kent TN11 0ZS
United Kingdom

or to the **'Sovereign World'** distributor in your country.

Visit our website at **www.sovereign-world.com**
for a full range of Sovereign World books.